FORGING A WAY

THROUGH GLOBAL LEADERSHIP AND TIMELESS SERVICE

A Historical View of
ALPHA KAPPA ALPHA SORORITY, INC.

Upsilon Kappa Omega

Compiled by

Desdy H. Paige, Historian
UPSILON KAPPA OMEGA CHAPTER

Forging A Way Through Global Leadership and Timeless Service

Copyright © 2013 by Alpha Kappa Alpha Sorority, Inc. Upsilon Kappa Omega Chapter
ISBN: 978-0-9914246-0-3
Library of Congress Control Number: 2014930386
First Edition
Printed in the United States of America

2 4 6 8 10 9 7 5 3 1

Cover Design & Layout by DNA Media
Edited by D. Renee Gibbs

Published by
Cranberry Quill Publishing, Inc.
111 Lamon Street, Suite 204, Fayetteville, NC 28301
www.CranberryQuill.com

Ivy Review Committee

Desdy Paige, Chair

Tracy Allen

Christine Campbell

Rochelle Carter

Dia Collins, Ex-Officio

Monica Mason

Arrie McAlister

Juelle McDonald

Sharon Taylor

Lyndelia Wynn

ALPHA KAPPA ALPHA SORORITY, INC.
UPSILON KAPPA OMEGA CHAPTER
EASTERN CAROLINA CLUSTER

TABLE OF CONTENTS

Dedication

This publication is dedicated to the charter members of Upsilon Kappa Omega who possessed the vision, foresight and desire to carry on the torch of "service to all mankind," a concept originating with the founding members of Alpha Kappa Alpha Sorority, Inc.

Acknowledgements

Upsilon Kappa Omega gratefully acknowledges its members (past and present) and their contributions to Alpha Kappa Alpha Sorority, Inc., the chapter, and its presence in the greater Fayetteville, Fort Bragg/Pope Army Airfield, North Carolina community.

Upsilon Kappa Omega appreciates the vision of its charter members for a chapter in the Fayetteville metropolitan area that continues the legacy of Alpha Kappa Alpha in its quest to provide "service to all mankind."

Gratitude is extended to members of the 2013-14 Archives Committee in its efforts and support in the creation of Upsilon Kappa Omega's first history book, *Forging a Way Through Global Leadership and Timeless Service: A Historical View of Alpha Kappa Alpha Sorority, Inc., Upsilon Kappa Omega Chapter.* Thank you to Carlotta Ray, Jacqueline Mardis, Sharon Taylor and Tracy Allen for your input, research and contributions to this achievement.

Thank you to the members of Upsilon Kappa Omega's "Ivy Review Committee" who reviewed and edited this publication at the chapter level. Thank you to Christine Campbell, Monica Mason, Shanita Wooten, Arrie McAlister, Sharon Taylor, Dia Collins, Rochelle Carter, Juelle McDonald and Lyndelia Wynn.

Finally, on a personal note, special appreciation and gratitude is extended to Upsilon Kappa Omega for its resounding support of the office of chapter historian and archives chairperson from 2011-2014. Your support has been an inspiration to learn more about the history and contributions of Alpha Kappa Alpha Sorority and share those "historical moments" at our chapter meetings. Thank you for your support in our efforts to preserve Upsilon Kappa Omega's history and legacy in print.

Sisterly,

Desdy H. Paige
Desdy H. Paige, Historian
Upsilon Kappa Omega

Preface

In over a century of existence, Alpha Kappa Alpha has established a rich legacy of sisterhood and service. From its founding at Howard University to its growth to over 970 chapters internationally, Alpha Kappa Alpha's story has been told by members who considered it an honor to write its history.

Jessie Roy, editor of the Ivy Leaf (1929-1933) was charged to write the first edition of its history in 1933 by the 7th National President, Maude B. Porter. Marjorie Parker produced the first edition during the administration of the 14th National President, Arnetta G. Wallace. After serving as 15th National President, Marjorie Parker produced four additional editions and held the title of historian until her death on January 16, 2006. Earnestine Green McNealey currently serves as International Historian for Alpha Kappa Alpha Sorority.

The Timeless History initiative was approved by the Directorate on November 5, 2010 under the leadership of International President Carolyn House Stewart, "a history major and advocate, to recognize history as AKA fundamental to illuminating AKA's very core and necessary for organizational and global recollection of AKA's essence." Under her leadership, Earnestine Green McNealey has been named to direct the Timeless History Initiative in addition to the traditional duties of historian.

Because history is important to the identity and perpetuity of Alpha Kappa Alpha Sorority, every chapter and every region has been charged to produce its history according to the standards outlined in several documents including Alpha Kappa Alpha Sorority's The Timeless History Guide. The goals for this project as set by Earnestine McNealey include (1) to tell the Alpha Kappa Alpha story through a coherent narrative that reflects authenticity, consistency and style (2) to leverage mediums for telling the Alpha Kappa Alpha story.

The *Mid-Atlantic Region: A Continuing Story of Timeless Service* is the publication of the region under the leadership of Mid-Atlantic Regional Director Linda Gilliam. It will be introduced at the 61st Mid-Atlantic Regional Conference in 2014. In this publication, Regional Director Linda Gilliam's goals have been realized: (1) to document the distinguished journey and accomplishments of the Mid-Atlantic Region (2) to complete and release a book of high quality printing with narratives and photos of all chapters in the Mid-Atlantic Region and (3) to present the book to the Mid-Atlantic Region in 2014.

In keeping with the goals of International President Carolyn House Stewart and Mid-Atlantic Regional Director Linda Gilliam, Upsilon Kappa Omega Chapter has established goals to preserve its history in print. The first goal has been accomplished; to submit an abbreviated version of Upsilon Kappa Omega's history to the Mid-Atlantic Archives Committee for inclusion in *Mid-Atlantic Region: A Continuing Story of Timeless Service*. The second goal is being realized with this publication; *Forging a Way Through Global Leadership and Timeless Service: A Historical View of Alpha Kappa Alpha Sorority, Inc., Upsilon Kappa Omega Chapter*. The intent of this publication is to tell the story of Upsilon Kappa Omega in a dynamic account of its chartering, programs, membership and vision including highlights of special events using photographs, news articles, an assortment of documents and other media. By telling our story, the history of Upsilon Kappa Omega Chapter, the community at large will be aware of the contributions and impact of our chapter in this great sisterhood. Telling our story in an evidenced based, stylistic manner will foster the remembrance, identity and perpetuality of Upsilon Kappa Omega Chapter.

Foreword

Upsilon Kappa Omega was chartered in a community whose characteristics parallels its own existence. Fayetteville/Fort Bragg, NC and other surrounding areas is a dynamic, transient community with a rich history. Prior to an established settlement by the Scots, the area was inhabited by various Native American tribes by the Cape Fear River. The Scots settled in two areas in the 1760's known as Campbellton and Cross Creek. These areas were known for trade on the Cape Fear River. African slaves, who later became emancipated freedmen also contributed to the rich heritage of the community; many established churches, schools and businesses in the area. Campbellton and Cross Creek were united and renamed Fayetteville in 1825 in honor of General LaFayette, a French General who assisted Americans in the American Revolution and who visited the area in this time frame.

As the area began to prosper, many other surrounding settlements or townships developed and are now considered part of the Fayetteville area. These communities established town governments and are now known as Hope Mills, Spring Lake, Linden, Eastover, Godwin, Falcon, and Raeford, North Carolina. Fayetteville is the county seat of Cumberland County in a community which now has a diverse population of over 370,000 people.

Fort Bragg was established as Camp Bragg in 1918 as an artillery training ground during World War I and renamed in 1922. The airfield at Camp Bragg was called Pope Field and renamed Pope Air Force Base in 1947. Presently, Fort Bragg is considered the home of the U.S. Army Airborne Forces, U.S. Army Forces Command, Special Forces and U.S. Army Reserve Command. As a result of the Defense Base Closure and Realignment (BRAC), Pope Air Force Base was merged with Fort Bragg in 2011 and is now known as Pope Army Airfield (Pope Field). Fort Bragg spans an area which includes four counties (Cumberland, Hoke, Moore, Harnett) including inhabited areas in the northwest area of Fayetteville and Spring Lake.

The Fayetteville metropolitan area has received The All American City Award three times (1986, 2001, and 2011). As a result of being a part of a military community, it has a diverse population with people who have origins from nations and cultures from around the globe. Fayetteville also has a rich history in education which includes three colleges/universities: Fayetteville State University, Methodist University and Fayetteville Technical Community College.

Alpha Kappa Alpha first emerged in the Fayetteville area in 1953 when Delta Alpha Chapter was chartered on the campus of Fayetteville State University. In 1955, Zeta Pi Omega Chapter was chartered. These chapters have established a rich legacy in service, scholarship and culture in the Fayetteville community that continues today. With its chartering in 1996, Upsilon Kappa Omega Chapter continues the legacy of Alpha Kappa Alpha with its diverse membership and dynamic presence in the Fayetteville area by reaching out to the Fort Bragg/Pope Army Airfield community.

Prologue

SPANNING THE SANDS OF TIME
UPSILON KAPPA OMEGA

The crest of Alpha Kappa Alpha Sorority, Inc.

The emblem of Alpha Kappa Alpha Sorority, Inc.

Prologue
SPANNING THE SANDS OF TIME

When as a student at Howard University, Ethel Hedgeman Lyle, before she had known a sorority, did conceive and present an idea to her friends. They, being women of strength, of character, and fortitude, came together in spirit and truth to support that thing which had been conceived.

It was the year of our Lord, 1908, when an inner voice spoke to them saying, *"Fear not; for that which is conceived in her is right. And she shall bring forth a sorority, and she shall call its name Alpha Kappa Alpha for it is the beginning and the ending of all Greek lettered women's organizations to come."*

So when the women heard this saying, they did bind together, and together they vowed to go out into the world and be of service to all mankind. The names of the founding generation of Alpha Kappa Alpha women are: Ethel Hedgeman Lyle, *Marjorie Hill, Beulah E. Burke, Lucy D. Slowe, Anna E. Brown, Margaret Flagg Holmes, Lillie Burke, Marie Woolfolk Taylor, Lavinia Norman, Ethel J. Mowbray, Norma E. Boyd, Joanna B. Shields, Alice P. Murray, Carrie E. Snowden, Sarah M. Nutter, and Harriett J. Terry.*

With the passing of years, these women became well known throughout the land. They were blessed and their seeds were blessed. Some became teachers, some preachers, some deans, and financial planners, business women, and community activists. Their accomplishments go on and on as they continued to grow and to multiply. In 1913, Alpha Kappa Alpha Sorority, incorporated as a perpetual body. Their bylaws were written on a tablet to be passed from generation to generation. Their constitution was ratified and the first national president was Nellie M. Quander.

Now the names of the succeeding national presidents are these:
Loraine Richardson Green, L. Pearl Mitchell, Pauline Sims Puryear, B. Beatrix Scott, Maudell Brown Bousfield, Maude Brown Porter, Ida L. Jackson, Margaret Davis Bowen, Dorothy Boulding Ferebee, Beulah Tyrell Whitby, Edna Over Gray Campbell, Laura Fife Lovelace, Arnetta McKarmey Wallace, Marjorie Hollomon Parker, Julia Brogdon Purnell, Larzette Golden Hale, Mattelia Bennett Grays, Bernice I. Sumlin, Barbara K. Philips, Faye B. Bryant, Janet J. Ballard, Mary Shy Scott, Eva Lois Evans, Norma Solomon White, Linda M. White, Barbara Anne McKinzie and Carolyn House Stewart.

News of Alpha Kappa Alpha Sorority, Incorporated spread around the world. Early in 1996, a war cry reached the ears of Doris Asbury who was the director of the Mid-Atlantic Region in the sandhills of North Carolina. It was the voice of Arrie McAlister crying out for help. In the diverse and growing population around Fort Bragg, there was found a need for an AKA chapter that could address and cater to the unique demands of the military community.

Along with Valeria A. Collins and six other dynamic Alpha Kappa Alpha women, an interest group meeting was scheduled. The name of the group was called *Harambee* which means *"self-help"* or *"pull together."* After nine months of organizing, planning, and selecting a slate of officers, the request for chapter consideration was forwarded to the National Office in the windy city of Chicago, Illinois.

Three months later, the AKA Directorate confirmed the efforts of the group and a charter was granted on December 1, 1996. The chapter's official name was recorded as Upsilon Kappa Omega. Subsequently known as UKO, it became the 108th chapter in the Mid-Atlantic Region.

The thirty-seven charter members of Upsilon Kappa Omega Chapter are:
Burma Valencia Anderson, Rochelle Delores Bethune, Lisa Thomas Boyd, Renarta Clanton, Erica Clemons, Carla Evans Collier, La'Shanda Collins, Valeria A. Collins, Patricia M. Corey, Shirley M. Evans, Shirley C. Greene, Angela D. Hinson, Althea Hurt, Lisa Jefferson, Sherrilyn M. Johnson, T'Anya Johnson, Robbie Richardson Lindsey, Arrie McAlister, Monique McAlister, F. Monique Kendall McCluney, Carolyn McLaurin, Wendy McManus-Gilmore, Barbara Melvin, Joyce T. Mitchell, Donna E. Moore, Angela J. Newble, Arnetta L. Porter, Allene A. Richey, Felicia U. Robinson, Cheri S. Siler, Beverly W. Simmons, Charlene D. Sumlin, Daisy M. Thompson, Valerie Wilder, Brenda J. Williams, Juanita Morgan Williams, & Twylla D. Willis.

The infant chapter grew and waxed strong. In 1998, another group of ambitious women were inducted into the Upsilon Kappa Omega family. They were called *"The FIRST."* *"The FIRST"* begot *"The Tenacious Ten"* and *"The Tenacious Ten"* begot *"The Teachy Two."* *"The Teachy Two"* begot *"The Eleven Enchanting Connections"* and *"The Eleven Enchanting Connections"* begot *"The Sweets Sixteen."* The *"Sweets Sixteen"* begot the *"Eighteen Scents of Sophistication"* and the *"Eighteen Scents of Sophistication"* begot *"'Til the End of Time."* In 2013, *"'Til the End of Time"* begot *"The Luxurious Eight."* And these are the generations of Upsilon Kappa Omega Chapter as they are known today.

Jacqueline Mardis
Upsilon Kappa Omega Chapter
"Tenacious Ten"

SPANNING THE SANDS OF TIME
UPSILON KAPPA OMEGA

Alpha Kappa Alpha
Sorority Inc.
• 1908 •

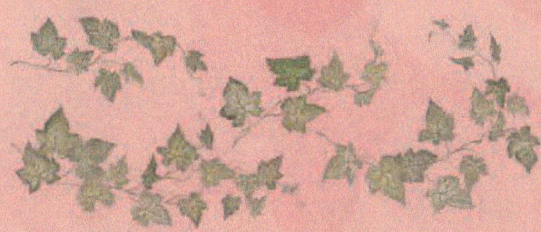

Introduction

PART 1

Introduction

Alpha Kappa Alpha Sorority was founded on the campus of Howard University on January 15, 1908. It was organized by nine college women lead by Ethel Hedgeman Lyle. In 1910, seven other women joined the sorority. The twenty founders of Alpha Kappa Alpha include the initial nine founders, seven sophomores and four incorporators. Alpha Kappa Alpha was incorporated as a perpetual body on January 29, 1913 because of the vision and leadership of Nellie Quander (one of the four incorporators).

Due to growth and expansion, the Mid-Atlantic Region was organized and established in 1953 from the South Atlantic Region and includes North Carolina and Virginia. Rose Butler Browne was the 1st Mid-Atlantic Regional Director. Under the leadership of Mid-Atlantic Regional Director, Dr. Linda Gilliam, the Mid-Atlantic Region celebrated its 60th anniversary in Winston-Salem, North Carolina in 2013. Two international presidents hail from the Mid-Atlantic Region: Dr. Barbara K. Phillips (20th International President) and Janet Jones Ballard (22nd International President). One Mid-Atlantic Regional director hails from the Fayetteville area, Dr. Marye Jeffries, 11th Mid-Atlantic Regional Director. She is a member of Zeta Pi Omega Chapter which was chartered in 1955.

There are a number of factors that have contributed to the growth and expansion of Alpha Kappa Alpha Sorority. Membership has its privileges including the bond of sisterhood. Upsilon Kappa Omega was chartered as the 108th chapter in the Mid-Atlantic Region on December 1, 1996 under the leadership of Doris Asbury, 13th Mid-Atlantic Regional Director because of the efforts of 37 charter members. The goals included expanding Alpha Kappa Alpha's presence in the Fayetteville area by extending services to the Fort Bragg and Pope Air Force Base communities, reclaiming inactive members and establishing outreach and services in the area. Perhaps Ethel Hedgeman Lyle said it best in the March, 1934 Ivy Leaf :

"...their loyalty to the pledge of Alpha Kappa Alpha kept the torch of our ideals lighted. It was due to them [incorporators] that torch lighted by us [founders] in 1908 has been passed to you..."

Ethel Hedgeman Lyle, Founder

ALPHA KAPPA ALPHA SORORITY, INC.

PART 2

Upsilon Kappa Omega Chapter

"UNITED WE'LL FORGE A WAY"
BEGINNING ANEW: INTEREST, ESTABLISHMENT AND CHARTERING

The year 1996 promised to be and was a wonderful year full of challenges, victories, and new beginnings. It was early January 1996 when Arrie McAlister and Valeria A. Collins first discussed the possibility of a second chapter in the Fayetteville-Cumberland County Area. That first dialogue between Arrie and Valeria resulted in the compilation of a list of thirty-nine members, some of whom were former members of Zeta Pi Omega chapter (also located in the Fayetteville area). This vision was also extended through contacts in local newspaper ads. Finally, in the spring of 1996, a meeting was scheduled.

Saturday, May 13, 1996 sent hopes and expectations to soaring heights. Valeria A. Collins, Arrie McAlister, Sarah Watson, Barbara Melvin, Daisy Thompson, Robbie Lindsey, Charlene Sumlin, and Beverly Simmons met for the first time to discuss the possibility of forming an Alpha Kappa Alpha Sorority interest group. The meeting was held at the Cumberland County Main Library with the following members in attendance: Valeria A. Collins, Arrie McAlister, Sarah Watson, Barbara Melvin, Daisy Thompson, Robbie Lindsey, Charlene Sumlin and Beverly Simmons. The meeting was facilitated by Valeria A. Collins and it was a wonderful beginning. Encouraged, the members in attendance outlined the goals for the group:

1. To expand the Alpha Kappa Alpha presence in the Fayetteville area by reaching out to the Fort Bragg and Pope Air Force Base population.
2. To diligently seek out those members in the area who are inactive and who would be interested in a growth opportunity.
3. To develop a plan of action.

A name for the interest group was selected from among several suggestions. During the discussion, it was noted that although the organization was founded upon the principle of college-level Greek lettered fellowship, it was also important to keep the link between the sisterhood and our African-American heritage. Thus, the name *Harambee* was chosen. *Harambee* is a Swahili word first coined by Jomo Kenyatta, means *"self-help,"* or *"pull together."* This was believed to be perfect in capturing the vision and togetherness of a group of women whose efforts were to support the growth of our sisterhood with determination, spirit, and unity while offering a helping hand to those in need within the community.

Harambee

"Here we are standing on the threshold of a new and great beginning.
Is it a dream? Is it real? Joy cannot explain what we feel!
Committed, determined, vision-filled are we of Harambee:

Committed to the teachings of Alpha Kappa Alpha Sorority, Inc.;
Determined to serve mankind with compassion and love;
Visions of greatness in service to our communities - Fayetteville,
Fort Bragg and Pope Air Force Base.
Here we are standing on the threshold of a new and great beginning.
Is it a dream? Is it real? Joy cannot explain what we feel!"

-Valeria Collins, 3/11/96

Confirmation of interest was no longer a dream because as time passed, attendance to meetings doubled! Enthused members were encouraged to continue to contact other Alpha Kappa Alpha women in the area. With affirmation firmly grounded and deadlines established for commitments, *Harambee* elected officers.

Harambee Officers

Chairperson: Valeria A. Collins

Co-Chairperson: Arrie A. McAlister

Secretary: Barbara Melvin

Assistant Secretary: Shirley Evans

Treasurer: Shirley Greene

Publicity Chairperson: Carolyn McLaurin

Hospitality Chairperson: Beverly Simmons

Parliamentarian: Mona Pollen

Harambee Interest Group

"PULL TOGETHER"

Fayetteville, Fort Bragg, & Pope Air Force Base, North Carolina

Harambee Interest Group Membership

Burma Anderson
Rochelle Bethune
Lisa Boyd
Renarta Clanton
Erica Clemons
Carla Collier
La'Shanda Collins
Valeria Collins
Patricia Corey
Shirley Evans
Shirley Greene
Angela Hinson
Althea Hurt
Lisa Jefferson
Sherrilyn Magby Johnson
T'Anya Johnson
Fonita Kendall-McCluney
Robbie Lindsey
Twylla Willis

Arrie McAlister
Monique McAlister
Carolyn McLaurin
Wendy McManus-Gilmore
Barbara Melvin
Joyce Mitchell
Donna Moore
Angela Newble
Arnetta Porter
Allene Ritchey
Felecia Robinson
Cheri Siler
Beverly Simmons
Charlene Sumlin
Daisy Thompson
Valeria Wilder
Brenda Williams
Juanita Williams

With the success and enthusiasm of the Harambee Interest Group, the names of thirty-seven members were submitted to the Alpha Kappa Alpha National Office for consideration. The Regional Director selected September 14, 1996 for the date to meet with Harambee. During the meeting, Harambee proudly spoke of its successful service programs in the community such as "Shower of Love" commitment, the "Operation Smooth Move" activity at Fayetteville State University, the "1996 Heart Walk", political activism, minority health issues collaborations, fund-raising endeavors, etc.

The official application packet bearing the names of thirty-seven members were submitted to the Regional Director, September 27, 1996. The AKA Directorate met November 2, 1996 and gave official confirmation of our efforts. A tentative date for chartering was scheduled for Sunday, December 1, 1996. The time for a real celebration of thankfulness was upon Harambee. The chartering date was confirmed!

Upsilon Kappa Omega Chapter was chartered on December 1, 1996 as the 108th chapter in the Mid-Atlantic Region because of the efforts of 37 charter members along with the leadership and approval of Doris Asbury, 13th Mid-Atlantic Regional Director. The lyrics of the chapter song, written by charter member Carla Collier, captured the excitement of this spectacular event: *"Salmon Pink and Apple Green, loveliest Colors we've ever seen; We are really making a scene, Sorority Queens!"*

The following officers were elected:

President: Valeria A. Collins
Vice-President: Carolyn McLaurin
Recording Secretary: Barbara Melvin
Assistant Recording Secretary: Twylla Willis
Financial Secretary: Charlene Sumlin
Treasurer: Shirley C. Greene
Corresponding Secretary: Shirley M. Evans
Hostess: Beverly Simmons
Door Keeper: T'Anya Johnson
Publicity Chairperson: Carla Collier
Historian: Renarta Clanton
Chaplain: Cheri Siler
Parliamentarian: Arrie McAlister (appointed)

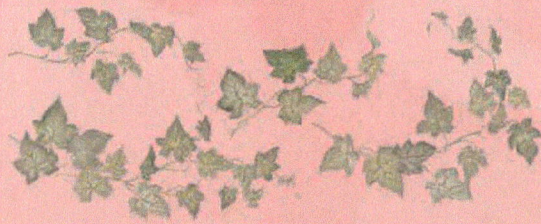

Upsilon Kappa Omega Chapter's
CHARTER MEMBERS

Upsilon Kappa Omega chapter's charter members are pictured with Doris Asbury, 13th Mid-Atlantic Regional Director (1st row center), December 1, 1996. News of its chartering appeared on page 30 of the Ivy Leaf, Spring, 1997 issue. On the top row left to right are Felecia Robinson, La'Shanda Collins, Angela Hinson, Monique McAlister, Sherrilyn Magby Johnson, Brenda Williams, Patricia Corey, Monique Kendall-McCluney, Renarta Clanton, Angela Newble, Rochelle Bethune, Shirley Greene and Arrie McAllister. On the middle row from the left are Juanita Williams, Carla Collier, Barbara Melvin, Lisa Jefferson, Wendy McManus, Valerie Wilder, Carolyn McLaurin, Daisy Thompson, Charlene Sumlin, Joyce Mitchell, Erica Clemons and Beverly Simmons. Seated on the front row from the left are Shirley Evans, Donna Moore, Burma Anderson, Robbie Lindsey, Valeria Collins, Doris Asbury (13th Mid-Atlantic Regional Director), T'Anya Johnson, Lisa Boyd, Allene Ritchey, Althea Hunt, Twylla Willis and Cheri Siler. Arnetta Porter (not pictured).

Chartering Ceremony

DECEMBER 1, 1996
Holiday Inn Bordeaux

Soror Doris R. Asbury
Mid-Atlantic Regional Director
Alpha Kappa Alpha Sorority, Inc.
cordially invites you to the
Chartering Reception
of the Harambee Interest Group
Fayetteville-Fort Bragg, North Carolina
on Sunday, the first of December
Nineteen hundred and ninety-six
at half after two o'clock
in the afternoon
Holiday Inn - Bordeaux
1707 Owen Drive
Fayetteville, North Carolina

RSVP   Luncheon Attire
(910) 868-2108 - Soror Robbie Lindsey
by November 22nd

The Chartering Reception Invitation

Alpha Kappa Alpha Sorority, Inc.
Harambee Interest Group
Fayetteville-Fort Bragg-Pope, North Carolina

Building the Future the Alpha Kappa Alpha Strategy · Making the Net Work

ALPHA KAPPA ALPHA 1908

Chapter Chartering Reception Program

Sunday, December 1, 1996
2:30 P.M.
Holiday Inn Bordeaux

Doris B. Asbury, Mid-Atlantic Regional Director
Valeria S. Collins, Harambee Interest Group President

Reception Programme

Denise Anderson, Presiding

Presentation of the Chapter

Welcome .... Mrs. Valeria S. Collins

Invocation .... Ms. Brenda Williams

The Occasion .... Mrs. Barbara Melvin

Greetings:
Lewis Chapel Missionary Baptist Church .... Dr. John D. Fuller, Sr.
Harry Hosier United Methodist Church .... Rev. Eldrick R. Davis
Fayetteville City Council .... Mr. Robert Massey
Cumberland County Board of Commissioners .... Mr. Thomas Bacote
2nd Support Command .... Col. Donald Porter
Pan-Hellenic Council .... Mr. Michael Bryant
Past President of Zeta Pi Omega .... Mrs. Eloise Haith

Musical Selection .... Mrs. Valerie Wilder

Recognition of Special Guests .... Ms. Beverly Simmons

Presentations .... Mrs. Arrie McAllister
Mrs. Donna Moore
Mrs. Lisa Boyd

Recognition of Visiting Greeks .... Ms. Renarta Clanton

Remarks .... Mrs. Doris R. Asbury
Mid Atlantic Regional Director
Alpha Kappa Alpha Inc.

Mrs. Helen Pierce
President, Zeta Pi Omega Chapter

Grace .... Ms. Cheri Siler

Harambee Interest Group Charter Members

Burma Valencia Anderson
Rochelle Delores Bethune
Lisa Delores Boyd
Renarta Dwaynyelle Clanton
Erica Clemons
Carla Evans Collins
Valeria S. Collins
Patricia McCamy
Shirley McLean Evans
Shirley C. Greene
Angela D. Hanson
Adilhea Hunt
Lisa Jefferson
Shawndyn M. Johnson
S'Anya Johnson
Fanita Kendall-McClenny
Robbin B. Lindsey
Arrie F. McAllister
Monique McAllister
Carolyn McLennon
Wendy McManus-Gilmore
Barbara Melvin
Joyce T. Mitchell
Donna E. Moore
Angela J. Noodle
Annetta Lattrice Porter
Adlena A. Quitcheny
Felecia H. Rochinson
Cheri L. Siler
Beverly W. Simmons
Charlene D. Samlin
Daisy M. Thompson
Valerie Wilder
Brenda J. Williams
Juanita H. Williams
Twyilla D. Willis

We, the members of Harambee Interest Group thank all of our families and friends for your patience, love and support during this endeavor. Your encouragement gave us the strength to meet all of the challenges we encountered. Again, thank you and we love you.

The Chartering Reception Program

Charter Members of
Upsilon Kappa Omega Chapter

Burma Valencia Anderson
Rochelle Delores Bethune
Lisa Thomas Boyd
Renarta Clanton
Erica Clemons
Carla M. Evans Collier
La'Shanda Collins
Valeria A. Collins
Patricia M. Corey
Shirley M. Evans
Shirley Greene
Angela D. Hinson
Althea Hurt
Lisa Jefferson
Sherrilyn M. Johnson
T'Anya Johnson
Arrie McAlister
Monique' McAlister

F. Monique Kendall McCluney
Carolyn McLaurin
Wendy McManus-Gilmore
Barbara Melvin
Joyce Mitchell
Donna E. Moore
Angela J. Newble
Arnetta L. Porter
Allene A. Ritchey
Felecia V. Robinson
Cheri S. Siler
Beverly W. Simmons
Charlene Sumlin
Daisy M. Thompson
Valeria Wilder
Brenda J. Williams
Robbie Richardson Lindsey
Juanita Morgan Williams
Twylla D. Willis

"To Capture a Vision Fair"

Alpha Kappa Alpha Sorority

To All Whom These Presents Come, Greetings:

This Certifies That

BURMA VELENCIA ANDERSON
ROCHELLE DELORIES BETHUNE
LISA THOMAS BOYD
RENAREA CCANTON
ERICA CLEMONS
CARLA M. EVANS COLLIER
LA'SHANDA COLLINS
VALERIA A. COLLINS
PATRICIA M. COREY
SHIRLEY M. EVANS
SHIRLEY C. GREENE
ANGELA D. HINSON

ALTHEA HURT
LISA JEFFERSON
SHERRILYN M. JOHNSON
T'ANYA JOHNSON
ROBBIE RICHARDSON LINDSEY

ARRIE MCALISTER
MONIQUE' MCALISTER
F. MONIQUE KENDALL-MCCLUNEY

CAROLYN MCLAURIN
WENDY MCMANUS-GILMORE
BARBARA MELVIN
JOYCE T. MITCHELL
DONNA E. MOORE

ANGELA J. NEWBCE
ARNETTA L. PORTER
ALLENE A. RICCHEY
FELECIA M. ROBINSON
CHERI L. SILER
BEVERLY D. SIMMONS
CHARLENE D. SUNLIN
DAISY M. THOMPSON
VALERIE WILDER
BRENDA J. WILLIAMS
JUANITA MORGAN WILLIAMS
TREECA D. WILLIS

College Women of ability and character have complied with the laws of entrance prescribed by the Boule and have been initiated into the

Alpha Kappa Alpha Sorority

In Testimony Whereof, the Boule on recommendation of the Regional Director, with the approval of the Directorate, hereby receives them as

Charter Members

of

UPSILON KAPPA OMEGA CHAPTER
FAYETTEVILLE, NC

having all the rights, honors, and privileges appertaining thereto

Witness: Our hands and the seal of the Sorority this ___1st___ day of ___DECEMBER___ A.D. ___1996___ .

Eva L. Evans Supreme Basileus
Linda M. White Supreme Grammateus
Doris R. Asbury Regional Director

City of Fayetteville
Office of the Mayor

PROCLAMATION

WHEREAS,   Alpha Kappa Alpha Sorority provides outstanding services internationally, nationally, and locally for the benefit of the public; AND

WHEREAS,   Upsilon Kappa Omega Chapter of Alpha Kappa Alpha Sorority embarks upon numerous local service projects such as, "A Shower of Love" - A commitment to the elderly, "Operation Smooth Move"--and activity at Fayetteville State University to welcome new students, the 1996 Heart Walk, collaboration with Interfaith Ministries to Feed the Homeless and a "Partnership in Math and Science"--a program in collaboration with Cumberland County Schools; AND

WHEREAS,   Alpha Kappa Alpha is the oldest Black, Greek Letter Sorority; AND

WHEREAS,   Alpha Kappa Alpha's target areas are Mathematics and Science Literacy, The Senior Residence Center, Washington D.C. Presence, A partnership with the American Red Cross, The Black Family and The Business Round Table;

NOW THEREFORE, I, J.L. Dawkins, Mayor of the City of Fayetteville, North Carolina do hereby proclaim this first day of December 1996

ALPHA KAPPA ALPHA DAY

in Fayetteville, North Carolina and commend this observance to our citizens.

J.L. Dawkins
Mayor

In recognition and in honor of Upsilon Kappa Omega's chartering,
Mayor J.L. Dawkins proclaimed

DECEMBER 1, 1996
In the City of Fayetteville

Alpha Kappa Alpha Day

PART 3
"Sorority Queens"
THE DYNAMICS OF MEMBERSHIP

The year 1997 was an open slate to be filled with memories beyond compare. The total membership committed themselves to the sorority abiding by its chapter bylaws, paying their dues and contributing to the Educational Advancement Foundation (EAF). There was a reinforced spirit of unity and determination – both needed to foster strong sisterly bonds while charting a new course of service in the community.

The Alpha Kappa Alpha woman has…*"the best that Womanhood in America can offer. They are women who represent high ideals, fine intellectual training, a wide variety of interests, deep experiences, and have made effective contributions to life of the nation in which they live."*
Edna Over Campbell, 12th International President

Because chapter members have diverse professional backgrounds including careers in education, law, social services/counseling, allied health/medical, real estate, military, finance and various businesses and entrepreneurships, transiency of the membership was both anticipated and challenging. Some members were military connected (active duty and reserves) or the spouse of military personnel. Military deployments were impacted by events around the globe. Other members moved from the Fayetteville area as well for job opportunities and promotions. Therefore, the membership rolls of Upsilon Kappa Omega (UKO) were constantly and dynamically changing on a regular basis. From the initial 37 charter members, the chapter roster has fluctuated from fifty members to over one hundred members. However, the chapter has faced the challenges of membership retention in a transient community.

Chapter Operations and Finances

Upsilon Kappa Omega operates soundly by the standards required by Alpha Kappa Alpha Sorority, Inc. under the direction of the Standards Chair at the regional level and beyond. UKO has been recognized at the regional level for submitting required reports and documents in a timely manner. The recognitions include being recognized as the "Best of the Best" in the region; the latest recognition occurred at the 2013 Mid-Atlantic Regional Conference in Winston-Salem, NC. The state of Upsilon Kappa Omega's chapter finances are sound. The chapter operates from an approved budget. Internal and external audits occur regularly. Efficient chapter operations and a budget that is financially sound affords UKO the opportunity to run the chapter smoothly and efficiently in order to carry out the business of the chapter and Alpha Kappa Alpha Sorority in the community through its programs.

Membership Intake

Desiring to expand Alpha Kappa Alpha's presence in the Fayetteville/Fort Bragg, Pope Air Force Base area by offering a life time opportunity of sisterhood to interested professional women with a history of service, academic achievement and high ethical standards, Upsilon Kappa Omega Chapter conducted its first membership intake in 1998. The newly initiated members were appropriately and affectionately known as "The FIRST."

Since the initiation of "The FIRST," Upsilon Kappa Omega Chapter has invited a number of ladies into the wonderful sisterhood of Alpha Kappa Alpha by conducting a number of membership intakes. Potential members had a plethora of skills to offer and received 'nicknames' reflecting the characteristics of the group as a whole and individually.

The FIRST	1998	Valeria A. Collins, President
The Tenacious Ten	2001	Shirley Evans, President
The Teachy Two	2002	Myra Payne Stokes, President
The Eleven Enchanting Connections	2003	Arrie McAlister, President
The Sweets Sixteen	2005	Cindy White, President
Eighteen Scents of Sophistication	2007	Dia Collins, President
'Til the End of Time	2011	Karla P. Dunigan, President
The Luxurious Eight	2013	Dia Collins, President

THE FIRST - 1998

THE TENACIOUS TEN-2001

THE TEACHY TWO-2002

ELEVEN ENCHANTING CONNECTIONS-2003

THE SWEETS SIXTEEN-2005

EIGHTEEN SCENTS OF SOPHISTICATION-2007

TIL THE END OF TIME-2011

THE LUXURIOUS EIGHT-2013

UKO chapter members with new members
(pink corsages) on September 29, 2013.

Upsilon Kappa Omega Legacies

Upsilon Kappa Omega is proud of members who are legacies. Arrie McAlister and her daughter Monique McAlister McEachern became charter members of Upsilon Kappa Omega. Former president Shirley Evans has three daughters who were initiated as members of Upsilon Kappa Omega: Sharla Evans in 2001; Chaundra Evans in 2003; and Christal Evans in 2005. Silver star Teresa Locus also has two daughters who have been initiated by Upsilon Kappa Omega: Courtney Locus in 2011 and Stephanie Locus in 2013.

In addition, UKO's membership also includes sisters who were initiated into the chapter. Terri Knight was initiated in 2001 and her sister, Walthea Corbiz was initiated by UKO in 2003. After Tamara Carter Woods joined UKO in 2000 (initated by Rho Omega Omega in Clinton, NC) her sister E. Rochelle Carter was initiated into UKO in 2005.

Teresa Locus (center) with her daughters Stephanie
Locus (left) and Courtney Locus (right).

The Jewels

Upsilon Kappa Omega, at its chartering was amongst the youngest graduate chapters in the Mid-Atlantic region and its appearance reflected the youthfulness of its members. At its chartering, the longevity of membership was less than twenty-five years. Carolyn Williams is Upsilon Kappa Omega's first one with membership of over fifty years in Alpha Kappa Alpha Sorority. Carolyn Williams joined Upsilon Kappa Omega in 1998 and is also a life member. Arrie McAlister was the first chapter member to become a silver star (25 year member) and life member. Other members later obtained the longevity of twenty-five years and the status of life membership.

Carolyn Williams: Golden and Life Member; retired educator; initiated 11/2/1953; charter member of Delta Alpha Chapter (located on the campus of Fayetteville State University).

UKO Jewels 2013 at the 60th Regional Conference in Winston-Salem, NC. (left-right) Desdy Paige; Cheri-Siler Mack; Arrie McAlister; Dia Collins (UKO President), Karla Dunigan, Juanita Williams, Arvita Callejas (seated) newly inducted silver star, (not pictured) Teresa Locus.

Silver Stars

Arrie McAlister-2004

Vikki Andrews-2005

Desdy Paige-2005

Cindy White-2005

Teresa Locus-2006

Cheri Siler -Mack-2006

Wendy McManus-2006

Juanita Williams-2006

Karla Dunigan-2011

Arvita Callejas-2013

Jan Johnson-2013

Lifetime Membership

Arrie McAlister – 2004

Desdy Paige – 2011

Karla Dunigan - 2011

The Presidents

Valeria A. Collins served as president two years after Upsilon Kappa Omega's chartering. In the early years following, the chapter president was elected annually along with a slate of other officers. Soon it was recognized that the dynamics of the chapter with the constant transiency of the membership, the need for consistency, the requirements for implementation of the chapter's programs and administrative matters, the bylaws were amended. The officers including the president would be elected every two years. Arrie McAlister was the first president to hold the office for two years after the bylaws change. Upsilon Kappa Omega has had remarkable leadership since its chartering. The presidents of Upsilon Kappa Omega have also served in various other offices and on a variety of committees within the chapter.

Valeria A. Collins
1997-1998

Charlene Sumlin-Cross
1999

- Chairperson of Harambee Interest Group

- Charter member of Upsilon Kappa Omega

- First President of Upsilon Kappa Omega 1997-98

- Initiated 1986 Zeta Pi Omega Chapter (Fayetteville, NC)

- Retired Community College Administrator

- Order of the Eastern Star, Past Grand Matron of North Carolina

- 2nd President of Upsilon Kappa Omega 1999

- Initiated June 1993 Sigma Iota Omega (Fairmont, NC)

- Charter member of Upsilon Kappa Omega

- Apprenticeship Consultant, NC Department of Labor

- Junior League of Fayetteville

Carolyn McLaurin
2000

- Publicity Chair of Harambee Interest Group

- 3rd President of Upsilon Kappa Omega 2000

- Charter member of Upsilon Kappa Omega

- Employed by Fayetteville Observer

Shirley Evans
2001

- Charter member of Upsilon Kappa Omega

- 4th President of Upsilon Kappa Omega 2001

- Retired Educator

- Three of her daughters were initiated by UKO

Myra Payne-Stokes
2002

Arrie McAlister
2003-2004

- 5th President of Upsilon Kappa Omega 2002

- Retired United States Military Officer

- Minister

- Co-Chair of Harambee Interest Group

- 6th President of Upsilon Kappa Omega 2003-2004

- Charter member of Upsilon Kappa Omega

- Her daughter (Monique McAlister) was also a charter member of UKO

- Initiated with Delta Alpha Chapter (Fayetteville State University)

- Retired Federal Government (Military Intel Specialist-Security)

Cindy White
2005-2006

•7th President of
Upsilon Kappa Omega
2005-2006

•Initiated Gamma Xi Chapter
(St. Augustine's College)
Raleigh, NC

Dia M. Collins
2007-2008 & 2013-2014

•8th and 11th President of
Upsilon Kappa Omega
2007-2008 and 2013-2014

•Initiated April 1998
Omicron Epsilon Chapter
(Elon College, Burlington, NC)

•Educator-Mathematics Coach,
Westover High School,
Fayetteville, NC

•NC Council of Teachers of
Mathematics

Sherrine Anderson
2009-2010

Karla Dunigan
2011-2012

•9th President of
Upsilon Kappa Omega
2009-2010

•Initiated Spring 1999
Gamma Gamma Chapter
Atlanta, Georgia

•Anderson Reality Group,
Real Estate Broker

•National Association
of Realtors

•Junior League
of Fayetteville

•10th President of
Upsilon Kappa Omega
2011-2012

•Initiated February 1986
Theta Pi (UNC-Chapel Hill)

•Silver Star and Life Member

•Employed by
AllState Insurance Company

•Society of
Claim Law Associates

Regional and National Appointments

In 2005, UKO member, Sharon Wilson was appointed as chair of the Eastern Carolina Cluster meeting held in Fayetteville during the administration of Mid-Atlantic Regional director, Ruby Batts Archie. Sharon Taylor served as financial secretary for the 52nd Mid-Atlantic Regional Conference in Fayetteville, NC. During her membership in Upsilon Kappa Omega, Vikki Andrews was appointed from the Mid-Atlantic Region as part of the Heritage Committee leading to the 2008 Alpha Kappa Alpha Centennial. In 2010, Cindy White was selected co-chair of the Mid-Atlantic Regional Conference (MAR). Members of Upsilon Kappa Omega have served on various committees at the regional level. The Eastern Carolina Cluster will host the 2014 Mid-Atlantic Regional Conference in Raleigh, NC. Appointees to chair committees include Karla Dunigan, who has been selected to serve on the planning committee for the 2014 Mid-Atlantic Regional conference. Dia Collins has been appointed as chair of the 2014 (MAR) Jewels Luncheon and Chekea Hinton-Mack has been appointed as chair of the 2014 (MAR) Welcome Committee. A number of UKO members have volunteered to assist and serve on various committees for the 2014 Mid-Atlantic Regional Conference.

Founders' Day Observances

Founders' Day is observed annually. Upsilon Kappa Omega Chapter observes Founders' Day annually and has served as hosts/co-hosts when chapters in the Eastern Carolina Cluster jointly observed Founders' Day in Fayetteville, NC.

In 1998 and 2004, the Founders' Day Observance for the Eastern Carolina Cluster occurred in Fayetteville, NC. In 2004, Upsilon Kappa Omega and Zeta Pi Omega (both Fayetteville area chapters), jointly hosted a Founders' Day Observance in which the International President Linda White attended. Upsilon Kappa Omega hosted a Founders' Day Observance at Gates Four Country Club on February 21, 2009. MAR Regional Director Caroline Lattimore was an honored guest for this occasion. Chapters from the area were invited and present for this Founders' Day Observance.

Ethel Hedgeman Lyle

Founders' Day Observance 1998

2004 Founders' Day Observance with members from Upsilon Kappa Omega and Zeta Pi Omega chapters.Seated on the front row are Dr. Caroline Lattimore, 14th Mid-Atlantic Regional Director; Ms. Linda White, 26th International President; Dr. Marye Jeffries, 11th Mid-Atlantic Regional Director.

Founders' Day Observance 2011, Gates Four Country Club, Fayetteville, NC

2009 Founders' Day Celebration

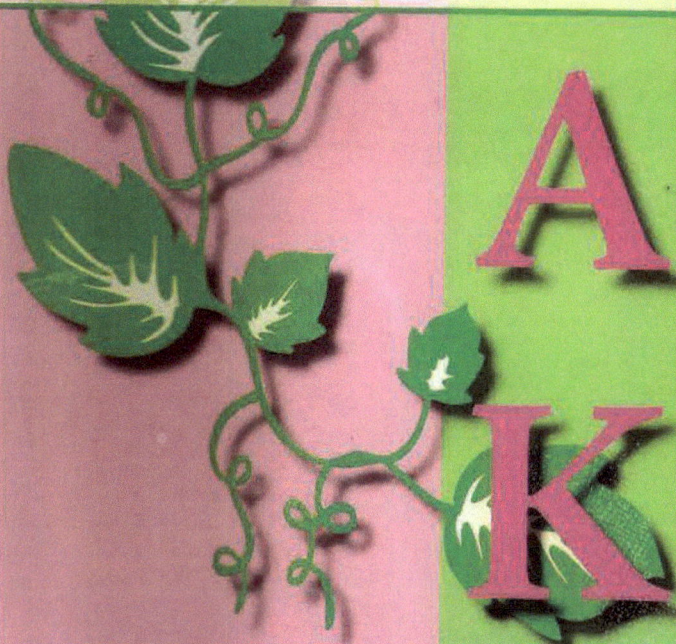

Hosted by:

Upsilon Kappa Omega Chapter

Gates Four Country Club

February 21, 2009

Founders' Day Celebration 2009
Alpha Kappa Alpha Sorority, Inc.
Upsilon Kappa Omega Chapter
February 21, 2009

Mistress of Ceremony	Soror Shirley Evans Founders' Day Chairman
Welcome	Soror Sherinne Anderson Basileus
Invocation	Soror Cheri Siler-Mack Chaplain
Musical Selection	Upsilon Kappa Omega Chorus
Presentation of Dais	Soror Celeste Bey Founders' Day Committee
Recognition of Special Guest	Soror LaTonya Evans Founders' Day Committee
Introduction of Speaker	Soror Sharon Evans Mid Atlantic Region, EAF Chairman
Guest Speaker	Soror Caroline L. Lattimore International Membership Chairman, 15th Mid-Atlantic Regional Director
Musical Selection	Upsilon Kappa Omega Chorus
Presentation of Gifts	Soror Connie Tator Founders' Day Committee
Grace	Soror Tanesha Hendley Founders' Day Committee
LUNCH (Entertainment)	
Rededication Ceremony	Soror Sherinne Anderson Soror Caroline L. Lattimore Soror Marye Jeffries Soror Sharon Evans Soror Cindy White Soror Mary Black
Closing Remarks	Soror Shirley Evans Founders' Day Chairman

The program for the 2009 Founders' Day Observance was printed on a fan.

The Eastern Carolina Cluster

Upsilon Kappa Omega is part of the Eastern Carolina Cluster; a geographical grouping of chapters in Eastern North Carolina.   In 2006, Upsilon Kappa Omega Chapter hosted the Eastern Carolina Cluster meeting at the Holiday Inn-Bordeaux in Fayetteville, NC.   Members of UKO regularly attend meetings hosted by chapters in the Eastern Carolina Cluster. In 2011, members of UKO attended the Eastern Carolina Cluster in Rocky Mount when a historical marker in honor of founder Anna Easter Brown was unveiled. In 2013, Upsilon Kappa Omega Chapter was recognized at the Eastern Carolina Cluster for being the chapter with the most members in attendance.

UKO Hosts The 2006 Eastern Carolina Cluster

Brigadier General Rodney Anderson provides greetings at the 2006 Cluster.

UKO members attend the 2012 Eastern Carolina Cluster in Jacksonville, NC.

UKO members are joined by Dr. Linda Gilliam, 16th Mid-Atlantic Regional Director (front center left) and Dr. Marye Jeffries, 11th Mid-Atlantic Regional Director (front center right) for a chapter picture at the 2013 Eastern Carolina Cluster (hosted by Chi Iota Omega) October 5, 2013 at the River Landing Club House, Wallace, NC.

A Collage of Group Portraits

UKO 2003

UKO 2004

UKO 2008

UKO 2009

UKO 2011

UKO members attend the 2012 Regional Conference in Norfolk, VA.

UKO members at the 2012 JOTT

Computer Workshop February 2011

Memorial Day 2011 in Veteran's Park

UKO members worship and fellowship together July 2013.

The Honorable Toni King (UKO Member);
Dr.Linda Gilliam, Mid-Atlantic Regional Director;
The Honorable Patricia Timmons-Goodson, NC
State Supreme Court Judge (AKA member)
at the 2011 AKA Day at the NC State Capitol.

UKO members with NC State officials at the
2011 AKA Day at the NC State Capitol.

UKO celebrates its 10th Anniversary December 2006
at the Ambience Entertainment Venue.

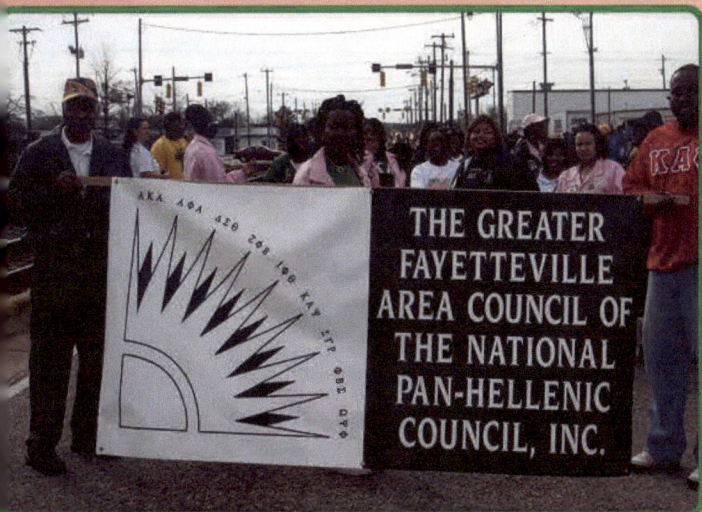

UKO marches in the MLK Parade with members from the Fayetteville Area Council of the National Pan-Hellenic Council 2007.

UKO member Angel Powell (far left) along with other Pan-Hellenic members at the 2013 Fan Drive.

UKO poses with other Pan-Hellenic members at the MLK parade 2013.

Upsilon Kappa Omega Chapter
IVIES BEYOND THE WALL

Floral Bearers
Women of Harry Hosier UMC
and
Somes of Alpha Kappa Alpha Sorority, Inc.

Honorary Pall Bearers
Members of American Legion Post 202

Active Pall Bearers
Men of Harry Hosier UMC

Ushers
Members of American Legion Post 202 Auxiliary

Acknowledgment
The Mitchell family expresses deep gratitude and profound appreciation shown during our time of bereavement. Thank you for all your kindness, thoughtful deeds and above all your prayers. May God bless each and every one of you.

Interment
Piney Grove UMC Cemetery
Maxton, North Carolina

Services Entrusted To:
Wiseman Mortuary, Inc.
431 Cumberland Street
Fayetteville, North Carolina

Obituary

Joyce Townsend Mitchell was born August 4, 1916 in Bronx, New York and died July 14, 1997. She was the daughter of Jean Townsend Gresham (whom she cherished very much) and the late John Townsend. She was joined in marriage to Webster B. Mitchell, Jr. in October, 1968.

She completed high school at E.E. Smith and graduated from NC Central University and received her Master's degree in Psychology from NC State.

She was a former member of John Wesley UMC and a beloved, active and faithful member of Harry Hosier UMC, where she held positions as Lay Leader, Financial Chairperson, Communications Chairperson, Church Secretary and member of Harry Hosier Mass Choir. Joyce was a member of Alpha Kappa Alpha, Inc. and past president of the Melvin Elliott Post 202 Auxiliary.

Joyce was employed at the N.C. Employment Society Commission for twenty-nine years and also as a Counselor for the Resolve Domestic Violence Program.

Cherishing her precious memory are two beloved god children, Alexia Michelle London and Cheryl Lennon; and a multitude of loving cousins and many, many friends.

She was understanding and compassionate and her legacy of kindness will live on in the great number of friends whose lives she touched.

Remember Me

Remember me not with sadness, now that I have gone.
From my earthly tabernacle to my eternal home
I didn't leave you, but I was changed
From mortal to immortal, rearranged
Remember me fondly with joy and love,
Now that I abide with my father above.
Earthly bonds which encumbered me,
Were shaken loose and my soul set free
Remember me when robins sing,
When the earth is completely renewed in spring
Remember me in the happy face of a child,
Recall fond memories every once in a while
Remember me in the rainbow God placed in the sky,
In the setting of the sun when night draws nigh.
It was all in God's plan, it was not fate,
And love is something death cannot separate.

Service of Celebration
For the Life
of
Joyce T. Mitchell

Saturday, July 19, 1997
11 O'clock A.M.
John Wesley United Methodist Church
616 Cumberland Street
Fayetteville, North Carolina
Dr. Jesse Brunson, Pastor
Reverend Eldrick R. Davis, Officiating

Order of Service

Rev. Eldrick Davis, Officiating
Mrs. Viveca Frye, Musician

Prelude

Entrance of Minister and Family

Words of Grace and Greeting

Hymn of Praise

Prayer of Comfort .... Dr. Jesse Brunson

Scripture Readings
Old Testament: Psalm 23 .... Ms. Jerline Miller
New Testament: St. John 14:1-4, 18-19, 25-27

Music .... "Order My Steps" ...... Harry Hosier Mass Choir

Acknowledgements

Obituary .... (Quiet Reflections)

Music ...... "I Love The Lord" ...... Harry Hosier Mass Choir

Word of Comfort and Strength ...... Reverend Eldrick R. Davis

Affirmation of Faith .... 883 ... "The Apostle's Creed"

Gloria Patri .... #70

Prayer of Thanksgiving and Acceptance

Viewing .... Funeral Directors

Recessional

Reflections

"Yea though I walk through the valley of the shadow of death, I will fear no evil for thou art with me, thou rod and thou staff, they comfort me." Psalm 23:4

On Friday, January 3, 2014, God in his infinite wisdom, visited Cape Fear Valley Medical Center in Fayetteville, North Carolina and closed the eyes of one of his faithful children. **Tina Michelle Graham Hawkins "Bean"** was born on November 18, 1967 to the late Glenn Thomas Graham, Sr. and Francina McNeill Graham in Fayetteville, North Carolina.

Michelle graduated from E.E. Smith High School in 1986, North Carolina A&T State University in 1991 with a B.S. Degree in Elementary Education and Fayetteville State University in 2011 with her Masters in Education. She worked as a teacher in the Cumberland County School System for 23 years.

Teaching and encouraging students were more than a career, it was her passion and life calling. While she was not blessed with children of her own, she spread her abundance of love by helping to nurture and love all of her nieces, nephews, godchildren and friends children as well as the children of the church. She was a member of Alpha Kappa Alpha Sorority, Inc., Upsilon Kappa Omega Chapter and The Order of Eastern Star.

A faithful member of Smith Chapel FWB Church, Michelle served as Youth Church Leader, member of the Women of Royalty Choir, Mass Choir, and Christian Education Department.

Michelle was preceded in death by: Glenn Thomas Graham, Sr. (father)and Gregory A. McNeill (brother).

She leaves the legacy of love to: her husband, Eugene Hawkins, Jr.; her mother, Francina McNeill Graham; three brothers, Glenn T. Graham, Jr. (Marilyn), Rodney Graham (Dedria), and Darrell Graham (Kecia); two sisters, Glenda T. McCormick (Anthony) and Sheridena Williams; three nephews.; three grand nephews; seven nieces; two grand nieces; three aunts, Vivian McNeill, Lynise Johnson and Luella McNeill; two uncles, John A McNeill, Jr. and John D. Shaw; god-parents, Willie and Betty Gainey; god-brothers, Keith and Kevin Gainey; god-children, Ashia and Adom Hembrick; mother-in-law, Callie Frances Hawkins; stepson, Julius D. Hawkins; seven sisters-in-law, Jeanetta Hawkins, Jennifer Hawkins, Jackqueline Spears, Cynthia Thomas, Sherrie Brown, Marlene Craddock and Sharlene Hawkins; and a host of other relatives and friends.

In Memory Of
Charlene Trezvant
IVY BEYOND THE WALL
June 5, 2011

Celebrating the Life of...

Charlene M. Trezvant

Charlene Marie (Hardaway) Trezvant was born February 3, 1969, in Chicago, Illinois to James Hardaway, Sr., and Katherine Marie Hardaway. She was the tiniest of the "Hardaway's bunch", but the one with the biggest heart. she was loved by everyone. Charlene was baptized at the Apostolic Church of God, Chicago, Illinois, under the guidance of the Rev. Bishop Arthur M. Brazier.

Charlene attended Drake Elementary and Cathedral High School in Chicago, Illinois. Some of her fondest memories of her high school days were with her best friends, Judi Terri, Jeanieene and Marixa a.k.a. "the most wanted ladies". She furthered her education by attending National Lewis University in Evanston, Illinois where she received a Bachelor of Science degree in education.

She was also a very proud member of Alpha Kappa Alpha Sorority Inc.

Charlene was employed with the Chicago Public Schools. She taught at Paul Revere Elementary School as a reading specialist for the primary grades where she was commended by her colleagues, parents and students for her passion of teaching. She felt like teaching was not just a job, but a "calling" and another way to serve God.

Charlene left Chicago to marry Aaron Dwayne Trezvant and moved to Atlanta, Georgia, where she taught second grade at the Albertson Elementary School in DeKalb County. Eventually she had to leave the teaching profession once diagnosed with kidney disease. She never complained and continued tutoring underachievers in her home in Stone Mountain, Georgia.

Anyone who knew her knows she loved to cook and entertain. Her BBQ was the talk of the neighborhood. Her home was always full of people, you could hear her laughter before you reached the door. In spite of her sickness, she was always ready to help anybody who needed her.

She found a new church home at the Green Forest Baptist Church under the guidance of Pastor George McCaley. When her body was able you could find her on Sunday morning, sitting in the front pew, singing and praising, giving her testimony on the power of prayer. In spite of it all her unbinding faith gave her strength to be a volunteer for the American Kidney Foundation.

On June 5, 2011 at the Cape Fear Valley Hospital in Fayetteville, North Carolina at 7:30 P.M. God whispered to her, "well done good and faithful servant. You have served me well. Come home, where there will be no more sorrow and pain."

Charlene leaves to cherish her memory: her parents James Hardaway, Sr. and Katherine Hardaway, brothers James Jr., Wayne (Yecki), Brian, sisters Darlene and Gina, nieces Tiffany Norwood (Michael), Christina Hardaway and Whitney Sol, nephews Bradford Lane and Christopher Hardaway, great nephew Michael Norwood, Jr. and a host of aunts, uncles, cousins, other relatives and friends. She was also preceded in death by her grandparents, aunts, uncles and sister-in-law.

~ Order of Service ~

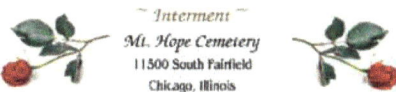

Organ Prelude	Bro. William Jackson
Processional	
Prayer and Scripture	Elder Clinton Hamer
Solo	Evang. Kimberly Hamilton
	"My Soul is Anchored to the Lord"
Resolutions	
Acknowledgements	
Remarks	
Reading of Obituary	
Solo	Evang. Kimberly Hamilton
Eulogy	Elder Clinton Hamer
Recessional	

~ Interment ~
Mt. Hope Cemetery
11500 South Fairfield
Chicago, Illinois

In lieu of flowers the family would ask you to donate to the
American Kidney Fund
6110 Executive Blvd. - Rockville, Md. 20852
1.800.638.8299

Pallbearers
James Crowell   Wayne Hardaway
Keith King   Bradford Lane
Joseph J. Freeman, Jr.

Honorary Pallbearers
James Hardaway, Jr.   Christopher Hardaway
James (Jim) Dorton   William (Preacher) Monaghan
Oliver Astley   Walter Astley, Jr.
Brian Hardaway   William (Wil) Davis

Sailing
You had been drifting, on a sea
That was relatively calm
For you waited for the right breeze,
To catch the sail.
On the horizon, the storm was arising.
The Gail Winds of life started blowing.
Before you knew it, an angle come to
Set the sail for a distant shore.
Although, the storm of life was raging.
It was very smooth sailing.
There was no more crying or wailing.
Elvie Patterson

Acknowledgment
The family wishes to express their appreciation for the kindness and sympathy extended to us during our time of bereavement.
Your flowers, cards, hospital visits, late night phone calls, hugs and prayers have been a blessing to us.
The Family

Brookins Funeral Home
9835 South Ashland Avenue
Chicago, Illinois 60620
773.233.3352
www.brookinsfuneralhome.com

Designed & Printed By Contance Chisolm (770) 621-9069

In Loving Memory Of

Born Into Time:
February 3, 1969

Born Into Eternity:
June 5, 2011

Charlene Marie (Hardaway) Trezvant

FRIDAY, JUNE 24, 2011
Prepast 10:00 A.M.   Service: 11:00 A.M.

Apostolic Church of God
6320 South Dorchester
Chicago, Illinois 60637
Dr. Byron T. Brazier, Pastor
Elder Clinton Hamer, Officiating

Service
TO ALL MANKIND

PART 4
Service to All Mankind
PROGRAMS THROUGH INTERNATIONAL INITIATIVES

Since it's chartering, Upsilon Kappa Omega has actively embraced and implemented Alpha Kappa Alpha Sorority's program initiatives inclusive of its own signature programs, scholarships and fundraising endeavors. In keeping with the Alpha Kappa Alpha tradition to be "supreme in service to all mankind," and to achieve program initiatives (including the 2010-14 initiatives introduced by International President Carolyn House Stewart), Upsilon Kappa Omega has partnered with a number of agencies in the Fayetteville area who serve the community through donations and volunteerism. The partnerships and collaboration include a number of area schools and agencies such as Habitat for Humanity, Fayetteville Law Enforcement Community for Operation Cease Fire, Second Harvest Food Bank, GEAR UP program at Fayetteville State University, CARE Center 24 Hour Safe Haven, Operation Inasmuch, The Bicycle Man, Hands That Help, the Angel Tree, volunteers with Missions of Mercy (MOM) sponsored free dental clinic, Salvation Army, Shop with the Sheriff and Stuff the Bus.

Upsilon Kappa Omega has also developed partnerships with a number of agencies who serve the community through various health awareness initiatives. The chapter has supported organizations such as the American Heart Association, American Cancer Society, American Kidney Fund, American Diabetes Association, and Lupus Foundation of America through donations, volunteerism and activities. Some activities include participation in Operation Smooth Move, the Heart Walk, Lupus Walk, Bowl for the Cure, Relay for Life, Blood Drives, Asthma Camp and Fair, and Let's Move (an initiative introduced by First Lady Michele Obama and America's move to raise a healthier generation of children).

In 2011, for Martin Luther King National Day of Service, Upsilon Kappa Omega offered its service to the Jubilee House whose mission is to provide temporary shelter, services, and programs to women veterans and their families. In July of 2011, members of the Upsilon Kappa Omega chapter volunteered in various capacities when this home was selected by the reality TV show *Extreme Makeover: Home Edition*. Upsilon Kappa Omega has volunteered thousands of hours in community service since its chartering.

Signature Chapter Programs

Upsilon Kappa Omega has been recognized for hosting sorority events, meetings and observances. Along with hosting/co-hosting Founders' Day Observances, Upsilon Kappa Omega was instrumental in the planning, logistics and hosting when the Mid-Atlantic Regional Conferences in 2000 and 2005 were hosted by the Eastern Carolina Cluster in Fayetteville, NC.

At the 2005 Eastern Carolina Cluster in Williamston, NC, UKO invited chapters to the 2006 Eastern Carolina Cluster in the Fayetteville area. The invitational, with its military theme was so successful, Dr. Caroline Lattimore, 14th Mid-Atlantic Regional Director, requested UKO's participation at the Public Meeting for the 2006 Mid-Atlantic Regional Conference in Alexandria, Virginia where its 'Tribute to the Troops' was well received.

Upsilon Kappa Omega hosted the 2006 Eastern Carolina Cluster in Fayetteville under the leadership of Ruby Archie, 15th Mid-Atlantic Regional Director. Greetings were received from many personalities and dignitaries in the community and the sorority including Brigadier General Rodney Anderson and the Honorable Patricia Timmons- Goodson, N.C. State Supreme Court Judge and member of Alpha Kappa Alpha Sorority, Inc.

UKO's "AKARMY" Salutes Soror Caroline Lattimore
2005 Eastern Carolina Cluster

Chapter Collaborations

Upsilon Kappa Omega has participated in joint activities with its "sister chapter," Zeta Pi Omega in various service projects in the Fayetteville area. Members of Zeta Pi Omega were present for the chartering of Upsilon Kappa Omega Chapter on December 1, 1996. Upsilon Kappa Omega Chapter and Zeta Pi Omega Chapter have jointly planned, organized and implemented events such as the 2000 Mid-Atlantic Regional Conference, Founders' Day Observance in 1998 and 2004 as well as the 2005 Regional Conference (along with other chapters in the Eastern Carolina Cluster). During the 2005 MAR conference, UKO sponsored the Ivy Reading Academy at Pauline Jones Elementary School in Fayetteville under the leadership of Dr. Caroline Lattimore, 14th MAR Director. Upsilon Kappa Omega Chapter was the host for the public meeting. The world renowned 82nd Airborne Band and cultural groups from the Fayetteville International Folk Festival fostered in the international theme for the conference.

Upsilon Kappa Omega and Zeta Pi Omega jointly participated in the Martin Luther King Day of Service in 2012 and 2013 and were honored to receive a regional grant to implement the service agenda for the weekend. In 2013, the activities for the weekend included the MLK Candlelight Vigil/March; MLK Parade, EYL Literacy Workshop, and a Sunday Supper lead by our Emerging Young Leaders (to Honor Veterans and Residents of Teague's Home for Women and Green's Home for Women).

THE FAYETTEVILLE OBSERVER • JULY 9, 2005   SATURDAY EXTRA

EYE ON THE COMMUNITY

Contributed photo

Caroline Lattimore, center, Alpha Kappa Alpha Mid-Atlantic regional director, and members of the AKA, Inc., Upsilon Kappa Omega chapter join Pauline Jones Elementary School students who participated in the chapter's Ivy Reading Academy. The Cumberland County school was presented with a $3,500 at the AKA 52nd Mid-Atlantic Regional Conference.

2005 MAR Director & Sorors of UKO
Sponsor Ivy Reading Academy At Pauline Jones Elementary

Women's Empowerment Seminar is an event that focuses on the empowerment of teens and women in the areas of self-help, finances, and health. Upsilon Kappa Omega sponsored its first Women's Empowerment in November, 2008. The event was held at Gate's Four Country Club. Local health providers and nationally known personalities such as Sybil Wilkes of the Tom Joyner Morning Show and Gloria Mayfield Banks, Elite Executive National Sales Director with Mary Kay, Inc. have participated in this program. These events were held at Dock's at the Capitol on Hay Street and Holiday Inn-Cedar Creek respectively. Vendors and health-care professionals participated and offered a variety of products, services and information relevant to the interest and needs of women and girls. In November 2012, the event was held at Gate's Four Country Club and two Upsilon Kappa Omega members were amongst the presenters: Sharon Wilson and Tracy Allen.

FLYERS OF WOMEN'S EMPOWERMENT SEMINARS

Jazz on Top of the Town (JOTT) is a cultural event sponsored by the chapter to raise scholarship funds while providing entertainment featuring locally and nationally renowned jazz musicians. JOTT has remained a popular sanctioned event of the annual Fayetteville Dogwood Festival (an award winning celebratory community event). The term Jazz on Top of the Town (JOTT) was first coined by Upsilon Kappa Omega's third president Carolyn McLaurin. As a sanctioned event of the Dogwood Festival, the first JOTT events occurred in a pinnacle room on the top floor of the Prince Charles Hotel in downtown Fayetteville in 1999. The first Jazz artist to perform was Reggie Codrington (professionally known as Reggie C.). The event's name was thus coined by the location and genre of music. With the growth and popularity of the event, the venue changed to a location nearby, the AIT building downtown where it was held for several years. N-Tregue (featuring soloist Carol Shaw), a group from Hampton, Virginia were the jazz artists who performed beginning in 2003 for the next four years. In subsequent years, other venues included the Crown Coliseum, C. Rose Agriculture Expo Center and the Ambience Entertainment Venue. Most recently, the entertainment venue that hosted JOTT was the Metropolitan Room in downtown Fayetteville.

Popular recording artists such as Art Sherrod, and The Jeanette Harris Band have provided entertainment. In 2013, JOTT's theme was "An Evening of Jazz at the Cotton Club" featuring the Deanna Jones Orchestra and DJ Sixth Sense from the "Russ Parr Morning Show." Many of the guests in attendance reflected the era of the Cotton Club in the attire worn to this event. Since its inception, JOTT has generated thousands of dollars in scholarships to deserving high school seniors aspiring to continue their education.

ALPHA KAPPA ALPHA
SORORITY, INC.

UPSILON KAPPA OMEGA CHAPTER
PRESENTS

an evening of Jazz

Featuring

DEANNA JONES ORCHESTRA

DJ SIXTH SENSE
-Russ Parr Morning Show-

8 PM -1 AM
ON
APRIL 27

Fayetteville
DOGWOOD FESTIVAL

THE METROPOLITAN ROOM
109 Green Street
Fayetteville, NC
For information, call (910) 797-1539 or
email ukofundraiser@gmail.com

WWW.UKOAKAJAZZ@EVENTBRITE.COM

The Ladies of Alpha Kappa Alpha
Upsilon Kappa Omega Chapter
PRESENTS

Jazz
ON TOP OF
THE TOWN
April 30th

9pm to 2am
Featuring Saxophonist
"Art Sherrod"

Experience an evening of Wine Tasting, Jazz, Dance, Food & Fun
The Upscale event you don't want to miss...

"Jazz On Top of The Town"
Featuring vibes by: Duplin,
Cypress Bands, and J. Wesley.

"Jazz On Top of The Town"
Saxophonist Art Sherrod

Hosted by
The Ladies of Alpha Kappa Alpha
Upsilon Kappa Omega Chapter
Classy Dress and I.D. required
Tickets are $30 and get more information

Ambiance Entertainment Venue
2510 Legion Road in Fayetteville

The Ladies of Alpha Kappa Alpha Sorority Incorporated,
Upsilon Kappa Omega Chapter.
PRESENTS

JAZZ
On Top Of The Town

Featuring "The Jeanette Harris Band"

APRIL 28, 2012 | 8PM- 1AM

AMBIANCE ENTERTAINMENT VENUE
2510 LEGION ROAD IN FAYETTEVILLE
Experience an entertaining evening
featuring Ms. Harris & a live Jazz Band,
Dancing & Light Refreshments.

Hosted by
The Ladies of Alpha Kappa Alpha Sorority Incorporated,
Upsilon Kappa Omega Chapter.

CLASSY DRESS AND I.D. REQUIRED
Tickets are $30. More information is available at ukoaka1908.com

VISIT WWW.UKOAKA1908.COM OR THE UPSILON KAPPA OMEGA FACEBOOK PAGE

Jazz On Top Of The Town

By Jennifer Milelli Mullen

End your Dogwood Festival frolic on a cool note with Jazz on Top of the Town, featuring national recording artist and Fayetteville native Reggie Codrington.

Watch the sun set on the Dogwood Festival from the top floor of the Radisson Prince Charles Hotel Sunday, April 25. Enjoy light refreshments and dancing from 6 to 10 p.m.

The event is presented by the Upsilon Kappa Omega chapter of the Alpha Kappa Alpha Sorority Inc. Admission is $10 in advance or $12 at the door and will benefit the chapter's educational scholarship fund, according to Carolyn McLaurin, event coordinator.

McLaurin said the new event was seen as a relaxing way to end the festival.

The UKO is a group of professional women who work to be of service to the community. Money is raised through a variety of avenues, including a Phantom Mother's Day Tea and the popular fund-raiser, the UKO Bachelors' Auction.

Current service projects include mentoring teen-age girls, volunteering at the local Care Center and offering etiquette workshops.

To purchase Jazz on Top of the Town tickets in advance, call 323-3950.

A Kool Carolina Affair
Jazz On Top Of The Town
April 25
Radisson Prince Charles Hotel
6 to 10 p.m.
$10 in advance, $12 at the door
323-3950

Cultured PEARLS

is a mentoring program for teen girls from grades 9-12 that encourages character and citizenship through service, education, scholarship, and cultural opportunities. This program was established in the first year of Upsilon Kappa Omega's chartering. Since its inception, a number of girls have earned scholarships to further their education. Participation in the program exposed teen girls to the ideals of Alpha Kappa Alpha. Kristin Pone, Christal Evans and Courtney Locus are three former Cultured PEARLS who later became AKA's and members of Upsilon Kappa Omega. Christal Evans (2005) and Courtney Locus (2011) were initiated by Upsilon Kappa Omega chapter. Kristin Pone was initiated at the University of North Carolina-Chapel Hill and later joined Upsilon Kappa Omega after graduating from this institution. Furthering their education and pursuing career aspirations have since led these former Cultured PEARLS and UKO members to other geographical areas of the country.

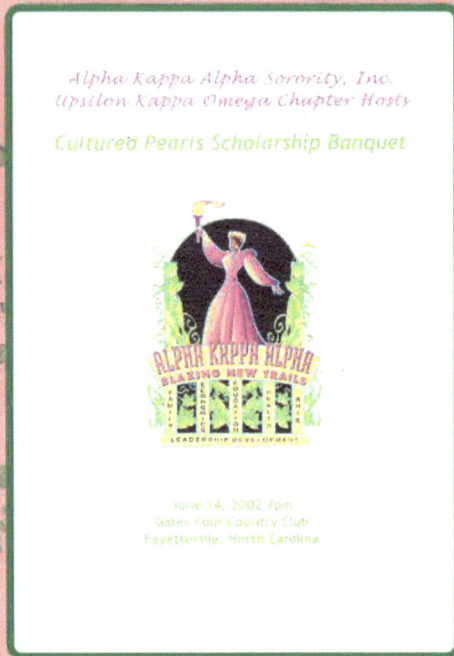

Alpha Kappa Alpha Sorority, Inc.
Upsilon Kappa Omega Chapter Hosts

Cultured Pearls Scholarship Banquet

June 14, 2002 7pm
Gates Four Country Club
Fayetteville, North Carolina

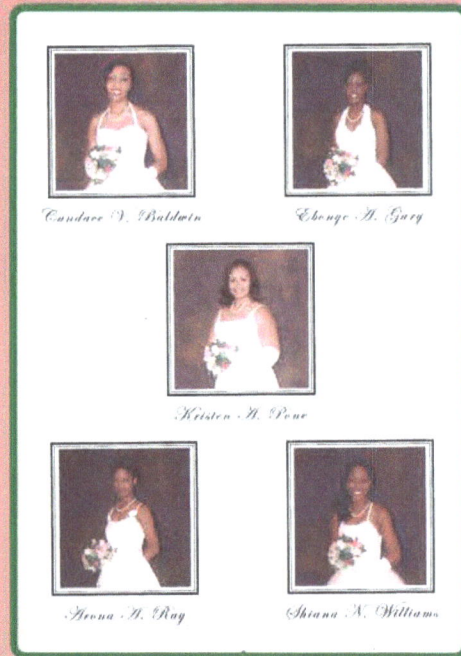

Candace V. Baldwin   Ebonye A. Gary

Kristen A. Pone

Avona A. Ray   Shiana N. Williams

Cultured PEARLS being
presented to society 2002

Cultured PEARLS and members of UKO
at the scholarship banquet May 2011

Scholarships are offered to deserving students who qualify and have aspirations to continue their education beyond high school. Upsilon Kappa Omega also remains an avid supporter of Alpha Kappa Alpha Education Advancement Foundation through its donations. Scholarships have been awarded directly to students and in one instance indirectly. Upsilon Kappa Omega donated money to the Tom Joyner Foundation in 1999 for scholarships when the radio program was hosted at Fayetteville State University. Students who have benefited from scholarships have participated in Upsilon Kappa Omega's programs such as Cultured PEARLS and through recommendations from schools and the community. In 2012, Upsilon Kappa Omega awarded five scholarships to deserving students from four high schools in the community. In 2013, UKO awarded four scholarships to graduating high school students.

UKO 2012 Scholarship Recipients

UKO 2013 Scholarship Recipients

PART 5
By Merit & Culture

PART 5

By Merit and Culture

CHAPTER AWARDS, RECOGNITIONS AND HONORS

Upsilon Kappa Omega has received numerous honors recognitions and awards from the community beginning on the day the chapter was chartered with the proclamation from Mayor Dawkins. It has also been recognized by the sorority in the Mid-Atlantic Region and at the national level. In 2009, Upsilon Kappa Omega received a Community Assistance Award for the Women's Empowerment Seminar. It was recognized at the 2006 MAR conference for its 'Tribute to the Troops.' At the 2006 Boule in Detroit, Michigan UKO members were honored to accompany the Mid-Alantic Regional Director, Caroline Lattimore at the Public Meeting.

UKO members with Mid-Atlantic Regional Director, Dr. Caroline Lattimore.
Golden Soror Carolyn Williams at the 2006 Mid-Atlantic Regional Conference.

At the local level, UKO is a life member of the NAACP and has been an active member of the local Pan-Hellenic Council. Upsilon Kappa Omega has partnered with the Greater Fayetteville Area Council of the National Pan-Hellenic Council on community service projects such as the fan drive held in July 2013. Upsilon Kappa Omega has been recognized for the various partnerships and service projects it has sponsored in the community such as Habitat for Humanity, Fayetteville Law Enforcement Community for Operation Cease Fire, Second Harvest Food Bank, GEAR UP program at Fayetteville State University, CARE Center 24 Hour Safe Haven, Operation InAsMuch, The Bicycle Man, Hands That Help, and the Angel Tree. UKO has also received certificates of recognition for its support through donations, volunteerism and event sponsored walks such as the American Heart Association, American Cancer Society, American Kidney Fund, American Diabetes Association, and Lupus Foundation of America through donations, volunteerism and activities. Some activities include participation in Operation Smooth Move, the Heart Walk, Lupus Walk, Bowl for the Cure, Relay for Life, Blood Drives, Asthma Camp and Fair.

2012 Heart Walk

UKO Goes Red for a Day February 2012

Hands that Help December 22, 2007

Read Across McNair April 2008

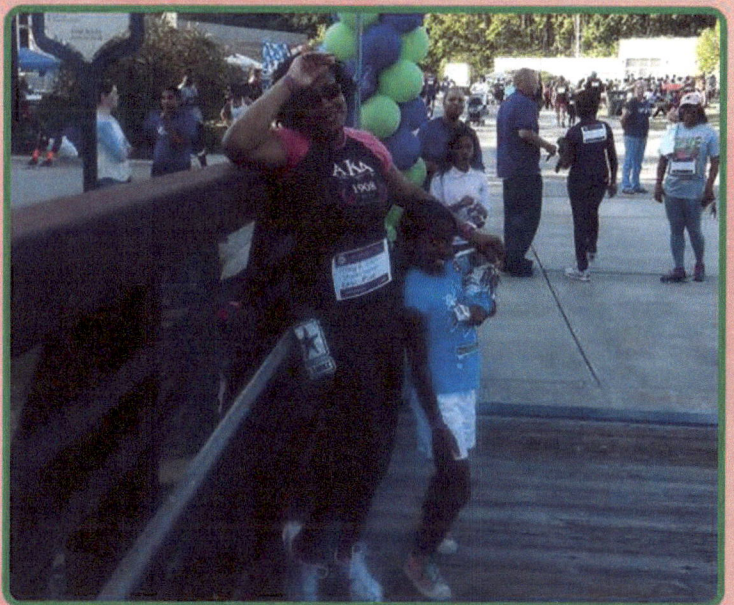
UKO members and friends participate in the Lupus Walk September 2013.

Voter Registration 2012

UKO and Cultured PEARLS volunteer for
Habitat for Humanity 2000

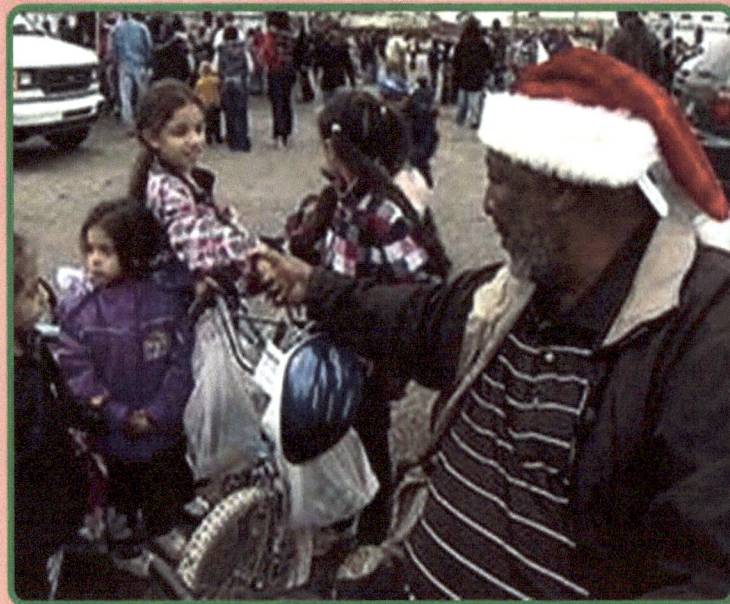

UKO volunteers for the Bicycle Man
(Moses Mathis) 2011 Give Away.

Bicycle Man Give Away, 2009

Extreme Makeover!

Fayetteville Observer, Published: 02:47 PM, Mon Jan 24, 2011

Cheers & Jeers for Tuesday, Jan. 25

Cheers and deep appreciation to the bold women of the Fort Bragg Chapter of Alpha Kappa Alpha Sorority Inc. The AKAs came en masse and filled the Jubilee House for Women Veterans with household goods and supplies, and the rest is history. The sisters of AKA led by example. There were homeless women veterans in the house who worked side by side with the AKA volunteers. Believe you me, they got a little stronger because these women showed compassion and concern.

To the leadership of the Fort Bragg AKA Chapter and to all who came (Brother Ques, also) and spent the day, you made a gargantuan difference in the lives of women veterans.

- Barbara Summey Marshall, Fayetteville

UKO volunteers at the Jubilee House for the MLK Day of Service in January 2011.

Members of UKO volunteer for Extreme Makeover Home Edition of the
Jubilee House in June 2011.

Members of Upsilon Kappa Omega have been recognized for their achievements in education, careers and for service in the community. Several UKO members have been recognized and received awards for their achievements by the Fayetteville Observer who sponsors "40 under 40 Honorees." These members have been amongst those selected because they are outstanding young professionals who are considered rising leaders in the community.

CONGRATULATIONS
40 Under Forty UKO Honorees

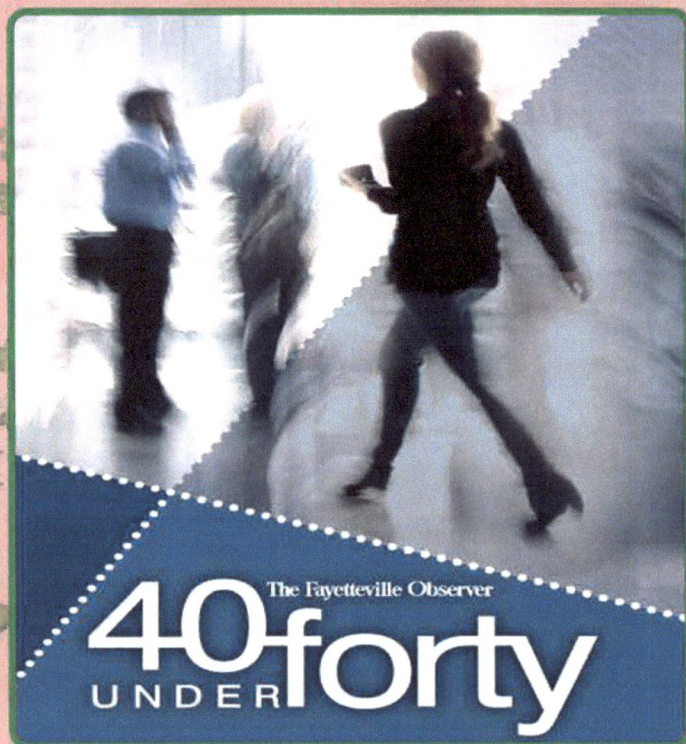

The Fayetteville Observer
40 under **forty**

Toni King-2011	Chekea Hinton Mack -2013
Kristen Braswell-2012	Sametris McKenney-2013
Juelle McDonald -2012	Lavondra Pye-2013
Andrea Royster-2012	Shanita Wooten-2013

Toni King 2011 Honoree

Kristen Braswell 2012 honoree
poses with her father.

Juelle McDonald (left) 2012 honoree
with a guest.

Andrea Royster 2012 Honoree (right)
poses with Monica Mason.

2013 Honorees Sametris McKenney,
Chekea Hinton- Mack,
Shanita Wooten, Lavondra Pye

Womack unveils the CaringTouch system

COL Vinette Gordon, RN

The nursing leadership at Womack Army Medical Center is proud of the military and civilian heroes within our organization. On a daily basis we witness the courageous acts of kindness and compassion the nursing team so humbly provides to our patients who are at the center of our mission.

The nursing staff's actions represent a powerful message of trust and encouragement.

The last year has allowed us to fulfill our unwavering commitment to our Wounded Warriors, their Family members, Soldiers, and beneficiaries.

We launched a patient care delivery system called the Patient CaringTouch System, a system that has allowed us to closely listen to the voices of our patients and our staff, as well as capture new avenues to enhance competencies for all nursing staff.

Our Patient Family Care Council has been very instrumental in recommending ideas that ultimately enhance our patient care. We are so thankful for the advice the PFCC provides because this consultation has directly influenced our patient and employee satisfaction.

Our nursing leadership team is extremely proud of the nursing efforts that are critical to the mission of Womack. This leadership team will transition. However, the care we deliver as well as the commitment we have made to our beneficiaries will continue to grow not only here at Womack, but throughout the Army Medical Department. We will remain postured and ready to assist our patients as they transition through our medical center. Thank you for your trust and belief in our nursing care. We are here to serve.

PHOTO BY CINDY BURNHAM

(From left to right) MSG Michael Pierce, SGM Michael Bivins, COL Gloria Bonds and COL Vinette Gordon

The Honorable Toni King was appointed and later elected as a district court judge in Cumberland County, North Carolina.

Colonel Vinette Gordon is recognized for her leadership as a nurse at Womack Army Medical Center, Fort Bragg, NC

Shavoka Douglas is promoted to Lieutenant Colonel April 2013.

Chelsea Forbes was sworn in as Attorney Forbes by The Honorable Toni King September 12, 2013.

In September, 2013 Shanita Wooten was appointed as assistant superintendent in charge of administration and technology for the public schools of Robeson County, NC.

More AKAlades!!!

• **Tamara C. Woods** received her PhD in Human Services from Capella University in 2013.

• **Benita Powell** was elected to the Executive Board of the Cumberland County Bar. She has also been inducted as an honorary member of the Order of the Omega.

• **Chekea Hinton-Mack** was promoted to Director of Operations for Johari Family Services.

• **Cheri Siler-Mack** is a Cumberland County Assistant District Attorney. She was selected as one of three recipients of the 2012 Champion for Children Award from the Cumberland County Child Advocacy Center. She was also appointed to the City of Fayetteville's Fair Housing Board for 2013.

• **Rasheeda Parson** was selected as Ms. 2013 Staff for Fayetteville State University.

• **Kristin Braswell** and her family were selected as the 2013 Fayetteville State University Family of the Year.

• **Patricia Bradley** has been appointed as the Police Attorney for the City of Fayetteville.

• **Audrey Noble** is selected as Hoke County School System's Assistant Principal of the year for 2009-2010 school year.

• **Dia Collins** was selected as Teacher of the Year for E.E. Smith School District and became a finalist for the 2013 Teacher of the Year Cumberland County Schools. She was also nominated by her principal for the prestigious Presidential Award for Excellence in Mathematics and Science Teaching (PAEMST).

• **Kathy Hardy** received her Master of Education from Liberty University School of Education in 2013.

• **LaVondra Pye** received her Master of Nursing from Liberty University School of Nursing in 2013.

• **Tenesha Henley** was accepted to the Curriculum and Instruction English Education PhD Program at NC State.

Upsilon Kappa Omega: In the News

UKO newsletter is formally given
a title in 2011.

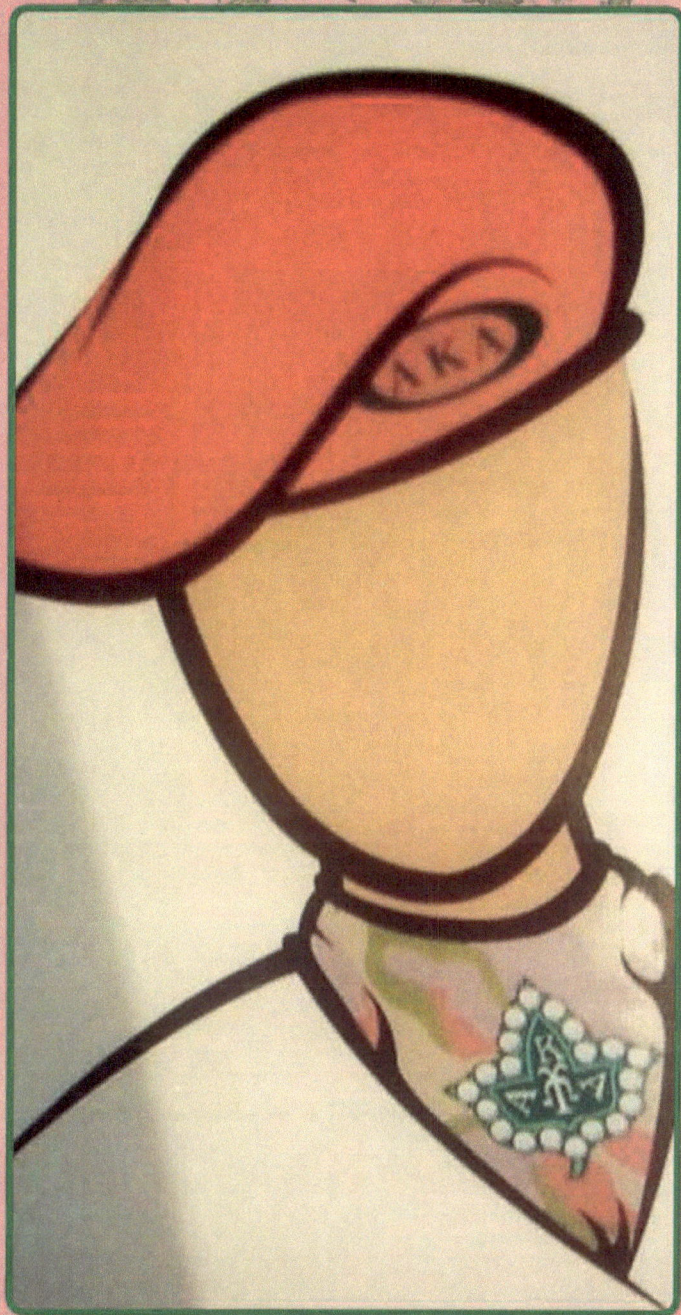

Beret Silhouette becomes
exclusive to UKO in 2005.

FAYETTEVILLE OBSERVER-TIMES
SUNDAY, MAY 2, 1999

Staff photo by Alice Thrasher

Charlene D. Sumlin, left, Reggie Codrington, Carolyn McLauren and Ray Codrington attend Jazz on Top of the Town, a fund-raising concert sponsored by the Fayetteville/Fort Bragg Upsilon Kappa Omega Chapter of Alpha Kappa Alpha Sorority.

Fund-raising concert jazzes up festivities

Sunday on the Square was winding down last weekend just as the Jazz on Top of the Town started warming up.

Young parents pushed their babies in strollers to their cars as jazz fans entered the Radisson Prince Charles Hotel for the concert.

Saxaphonist **Reggie Codrington** got help from his dad, **Ray Codrington,** to play the concert in the top-floor ballroom. The proud father announced that Reggie's new album with Mylestone Records will be released soon.

The concert was sponsored by the Fayetteville/Fort Bragg Upsilon Kappa Omega Chapter of Alpha Kappa Alpha Sorority.

Carolyn McLaurin, head of the fund-raising committee, says proceeds from the concert tickets go to the service organization's scholarship fund.

She and chapter president **Charlene Sumlin** and other members greeted the guests as they entered the ballroom for the 6 p.m. social period before the performance began.

Staff photo by Jay Capers

Alpha Kappa Alpha sorority, Upsilon Kappa Omega chapter recently welcomed new members. Welcoming them are Valeria Collins, front row left, president; Shirley Greene, vice president; and Shirley Evans, membership chair. New members are Fitilma Muhammad, Lyndelia Wynn, Lesley Brickhouse, Robin Browder-Swinson, Dionne Hall and Kathey Willis. On the back row from the left are Revella Lynn Surles, Michelle Graham, Xaviera Williams, Beth A. Hall, Anne Brinkley, Jeanette Avery, Barbra Parker and Angela S. Whitson.

EYE ON THE COMMUNITY

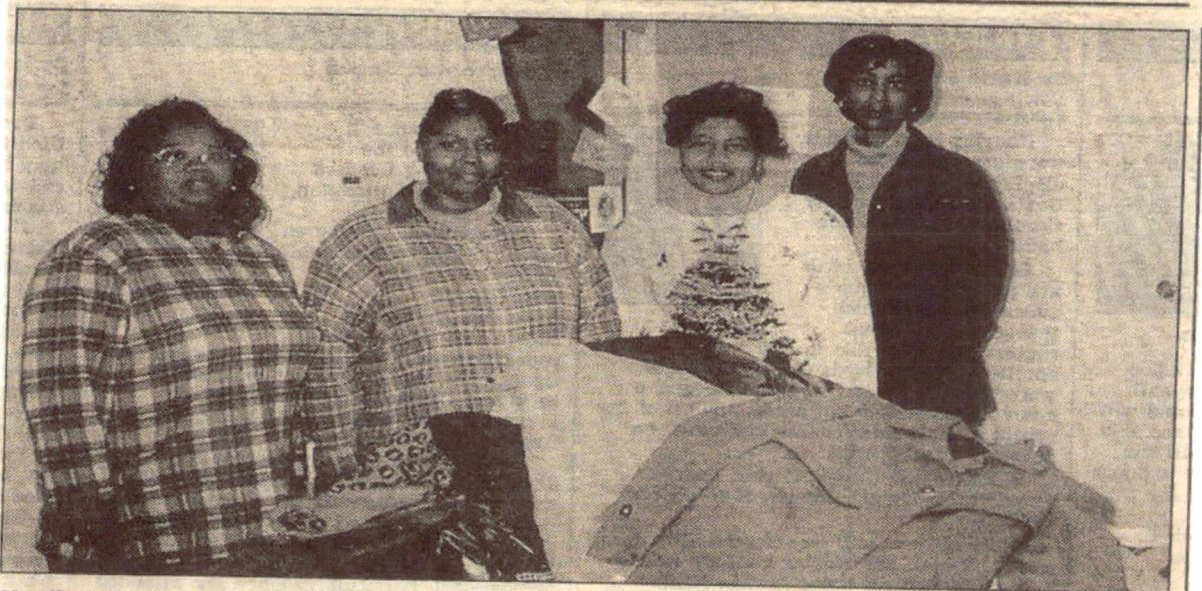

Upsilon Kappa Omega chapter of Alpha Kappa Alpha sorority members recently donated more than 100 coats to Fayetteville Urban Ministry. From left to right are Lyndelia Wynn, Sherry Gamble, who is emergency assistance coordinator for the ministry, Shirley Evans and Angela Whitson.

Staff photo by Swayne Hall

Sisters of Upsilon Kappa Omega are, top row left to right, Felecia Robinson, La'Shanda Collins, Angela Hinson, Monique McAlister, Sherrilyn Johnson, Brenda Williams, Patricia Corey, Monique Kendall-McCluney, Renarta Clanton, Angela Newble, Rochelle Bethune, Shirley Greene and Arrie McAlister. On the middle row from left are Juanita Williams, Carla Collier, Barbara Melvin, Lisa Jefferson, Wendy McManus, Valerie Wilder, Carolyn McLaurin, Daisy Thompson, Charlene Sumlin, Joyce Mitchell, Erica Clemons and Beverly Simmons. Seated on the front row from the left are Shirley Evans, Donna Moore, Burmna Anderson, Robbie Lindsey, Veleria Collins, Doris Asbury, T'Anya Johnson, Lisa Boyd, Allene Ritchey, Althea Hurt, Twylla Willis and Cherie Siler. Arnetta Porte, not pictured, is a member of the sorority.

Pulling together.

Sorority's newest chapter turns to military population

By Karen LaCaire Bouvier
Correspondent

Alpha Kappa Alpha, a national sorority dedicated to community service and better education, recently chartered its 108th chapter in the Mid Atlantic region, which includes North Carolina and Virginia.

The Fayetteville chapter will be known as Upsilon Kappa Omega and is the second chapter in Fayetteville. Zeta Pi Omega chapter has been here since 1955. Alpha Kappa Alpha was founded in 1908, and has more than 80,000 members nationally.

"But we wanted a chapter that would especially target our vast population here at Fort Bragg and Pope Air Force Base," Arrie McCallister, founder of the new chapter, said. "We realized there were large numbers of inactive former members in the military community here that would be interested in being active in the wonderful accomplishments of Alpha Kappa Alpha."

McCallister, a member of the sorority since 1974, when she joined the Fayetteville State University Delta Alpha chapter, began organizing an interest group to

'We look forward to doing great work in this community.'

— *Veleria Collins*

establish the new chapter in January. She enlisted the aid of active member Veleria Collins, a graduate member of the Beta Phi Omega chapter since 1986.

"We wanted to encourage women who were affiliated with the military to feel more a part of this organization," said Collins, a military wife. "These women who move around a lot have very diverse interests and contacts. We felt there were enough of us to make a real difference in affecting the programmatic thrusts, goals and objectives of the sorority."

The interest group, which had been known as Harambee, a Swahili concept meaning "to pull together," was chartered as Upsilon Kappa Omega with 37 initial members. More than 150 people helped celebrate the chartering at a ceremony and reception on Nov. 30 at the

Holiday Inn Bordeaux.

"We look forward to doing great work in this community," Collins said. "We will begin with three major goals starting with a program in the Fort Bragg schools, which will center on enhancing children's math and science skills."

The group's second goal is to develop a partnership with the Red Cross in an effort to look at minority health issues, and the members will conduct a "shower of love" outreach to the elderly in area nursing homes.

The third goal, amid a longer list of objectives, is a bone marrow drive in conjunction with Fayetteville Technical Community College, which will be held at the school on Feb. 13.

"We invite inquiries and hope to motivate other former members in the area to join us," Collins said, noting that one charter member is serving as a military liaison at Fort Bragg. "Donna Moore is a captain in the (Army) Nurses Corps and we are very happy to have her to help with our future goals to recruit, retain and reclaim our inactive members."

Those interested in joining the new chapter can contact Collins at 867-1961.

Lumberton, N.C.   Established 1870   www.robesonian.com   Civitas Media, LLC   All Rights Reserved

THE ROBESONIAN

Wednesday
July 10, 2013
Volume 144 No. 87

Daily   Sunday
50¢ $1.50

Schools cleared on catering

Lawyer: Hunt didn't steer business

Bob Shiles
Kelly Mayo
Staff writers

LUMBERTON — The Public Schools of Robeson County has not violated state law when spending public money for catering services with a business owned and operated by the superintendent's wife's family, an independent attorney told the Board of Education on Tuesday.

Nick Sojka, the attorney for the school boards in Hoke and Scotland counties, also said that Superintendent Johnny Hunt has not been involved in drafting or administering any catering contracts entered into by the school district, and that the recent creation of a new catering company by Hunt's brother-in-law, separate from Fuller's Barbecue, will allow the school district to use a Fuller's-associated company

without fear of violating state laws or ethics.

"Based upon my review of documentation and interviews, I don't believe there has been any violation of state law," said Sojka, who was hired last month by the school board to review the local school system's procedures for hiring caterers. "I did not see any extravagant expense that could not be

See **CLEARED | 5A**

ck Sojka

Kelly Mayo | The Robesonian

Rowland Middle School Principal Shanita Wooten, center, accepts the award for middle school attendance with Superintendent Johnny Hunt, left, and Board Chairman Loistine DeFreece. Rowland Middle achieved 97.85 percent attendance during the 2012-13 school year.

Bird in hand

Rowland to close rail tracks

Shanita Wooten (center, top right) accepts the award for middle school attendance (Rowland Middle School) in Robeson County, N.C.

The Social Scene

Upsilon Kappa Omega has hosted a number of social events and activities in the Fayetteville/Fort Bragg/Pope Field community for the purpose of socializing, networking, collaborating, and fellowship. Ultimately, many of the events have been fundraisers to support UKO's various programs and scholarship efforts. The community has supported Upsilon Kappa Omega in its efforts with attendance to various events and financial support through sponsorship. Members have found enjoyment socializing with citizens in the community and with one another.

Alpha Kappa Alpha Sorority, Inc.
Upsilon Kappa Omega Chapter

Charity Bachelor Auction '97
Theme: A Few Good Men...

November 15, 1997
Six O'Clock in the Evening
Radisson Prince Charles Hotel
Fayetteville, North Carolina

ALPHA KAPPA ALPHA
SORORITY INC.
UPSILON KAPPA OMEGA CHAPTER
PRESENTS

an evening of Jazz
AT THE COTTON CLUB

APRIL 27, 2013
METROPOLITAN ROOM
8:00PM

TICKET PRICE
$35.00
(IN ADVANCE)

All proceeds will benefit the sorority's scholarships and community programs

featuring The Deanna Jones Orchestra
& DJ Sixth Sense from "The Russ Parr Morning Show"
For tickets email: UKOFundraiser@gmail.com or
www.Eventbrite.com

Alpha Kappa Alpha Sorority, Inc.
Upsilon Kappa Omega Chapter
Proudly Presents

A MaskAKArade
Saturday - November 19, 2011
Pierro's Italian Bistro Sky Lounge
217 Hay Street - Fayetteville, NC
10:00 p.m. - 1:00 a.m.

Proceeds goes to Upsilon Kappa Omega's Scholarships & Community Efforts

Donation: $10.00

Alpha Kappa Alpha Sorority, Inc.
Upsilon Kappa Omega Chapter
Proudly presents

"Pearl Jam"

Friday
September 21, 2012
9:00 p.m. - 1:00 a.m.
Metropolitan Room
109 Green Street
Fayetteville, North Carolina 28301

Casual Dress

Donation: $20.00

35% sends to support Upsilon Kappa Omega's Scholarship Fund

Alpha Kappa Alpha Sorority, Inc.
Upsilon Kappa Omega Chapter
Proudly presents
"Pearl Jam"

Proceeds to support
Upsilon Kappa Omega's Scholarship Fund
Where: Metropolitan Room
109 Green Street Fayetteville, NC 28301
Date: Friday September 21, 2012
Party: 9:00 p.m.-1:00 am
Dress Code: Casual
Cost: $20

Tickets can be purchased from a member of the UKO

Website at www.akaUKO.com, or UKO Facebook page

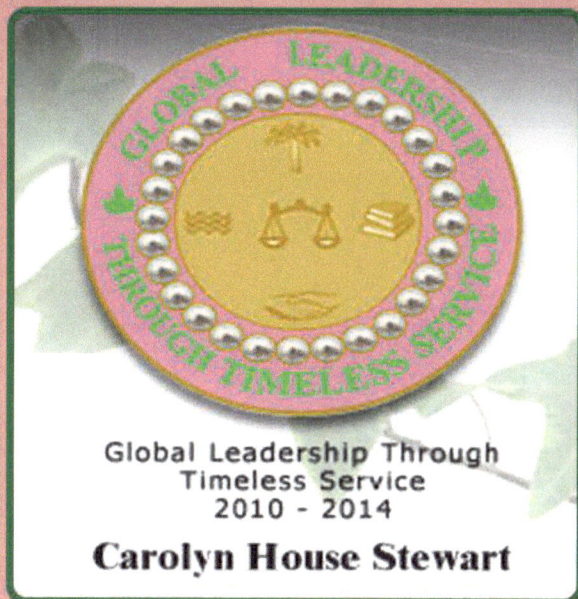

Global Leadership Through
Timeless Service
2010 - 2014
Carolyn House Stewart

PART 6

The Era of Global Leadership Through Timeless Service

In keeping with the Alpha Kappa Alpha tradition to be "supreme in service to all mankind," and to achieve the 2010-14 program initiatives introduced by International President Carolyn House Stewart, Upsilon Kappa Omega has implemented a number of programs, events and activities in the Fayetteville/Fort Bragg area. Some of these programs include collaboration with agencies who also serve the community. The purpose of the program initiatives are "inspired by a dedicated investment of human capital and a bold commitment to the principles of basic human rights." Upsilon Kappa Omega Chapter along with all chapters of Alpha Kappa Alpha Sorority was invited to accept the mission of "global leadership through timeless service" at the beginning of the administration of International President Carolyn House Stewart. Chapters were challenged to "devote [their] talent and resources, [the] causes of awareness, advocacy and action [as] the primary vehicles for the worldwide delivery of service initiatives." The signature program initiatives are as follows:

1. Emerging Young Leaders (EYL) Initiatives. This program impacts the lives of 10,000 girls in grades six through eight by providing leadership development, civic engagement, enhanced academic preparation and character building. Upsilon Kappa Omega Chapter launched the EYL program September 2011 with an introductory meeting. The program started in September at Reid Ross Classical School for 6-8 grade girls meeting a minimal of once per month. At the end June of 2012 and 2013, girls who had successfully completed the program where acknowledged through a "graduation." At the 2013 Mid-Atlantic Regional Conference in Winston-Salem, EYL girls from Upsilon Kappa Omega Chapter and Zeta Pi Omega Chapter were recognized at the Public meeting at the beginning of the conference by Dr. Linda Gilliam, Mid-Atlantic Regional Director.

II. Health Initiatives- These initiatives encourage personal fitness and healthy lifestyles by supporting organizations which advance access to treatment and coordinate awareness and advocacy campaigns to reduce health disparities, save lives and impact health related legislation. Co-sponsored health forums address diseases which disproportionately affect women and minorities, prevention and treatment options. Between 2011-13, Upsilon Kappa Omega Chapter has sponsored, hosted, collaborated or donated to Project Let's Move (with a focus on healthy eating for children, childhood diabetes and exercising), the Heart Walk, donation to American Kidney Foundation, Heifer International, blood drive, volunteerism at the Salvation Army shelter, Missions of Mercy (MOM) sponsored free dental clinic, and the Lupus Walk.

A. Asthma Prevention and Management Initiative. The purpose of this health program is diagnosis, treatment awareness and parental education and advocacy. Between 2011-13, Upsilon Kappa Omega Chapter has partnered with the Cumberland County Asthma Action group, Asthma Fair and Asthma Camp.

B. Environmental Stewardship and Sustainability. Through community forums and activities, this initiative promotes strategies and awareness campaigns that encourage energy efficiency, conservation, eco-living, reforestation, urban gardening, education and empowerment of consumers with limited resources, "go green-living green" eco-tourism, opportunities for women owned businesses, environmental zones in urban communities and advocacy for and legislation related to public health and environmental justice. Upsilon Kappa Omega Chapter has progressed in the area of "go green-living green" by utilizing technology in all aspects of chapter operations. The chapter uses computer technology to communicate with members on a regular and consistent basis. In February 2011, the technology committee hosted a workshop for members to get acclimated to using technology for chapter operations and for personal use. The monthly chapter newsletter has been disseminated online for several years. UKO has also had a functioning website for a number of years. In 2011, under the leadership of Karla Dunigan and guidance from then editor Lydia Berrios, the newsletter was formally given a name: ***The Ivy View.*** Under the guidance of technology chair and webmaster Angel Powell, UKO's chapter website has been updated and deemed the 41st chapter in the Mid-Atlantic Region as 100% compliant as indicated in an email from the MAR Technology chairperson on March 25, 2013; and a Facebook page has also been created. Along with "going green, living green" these efforts increase communication amongst chapter members and provide general information about the chapter, it's activities, events and programs to the community.

III. Global Poverty-The goals for this initiative are to end hunger, preserve the environment and empower women. This program provides food production skills and training in self-reliance through gifts of seeds, livestock and training in environmentally sound agriculture. Between 2010-13, Upsilon Kappa Omega Chapter has donated to the 2nd Harvest Food Bank, provided a mini Makeover of Jubilee House for Women Veterans and their families, participated in Extreme Makeover of the Jubilee House, and participated in a shoe drive.

IV. Economic Security Initiative-This effort expands the current programs related to wealth building and allocation of resources, home ownership, estate planning, support and empowerment of female owned businesses and urban enterprise zones. Between 2010-13 Upsilon Kappa Omega Chapter has sponsored the STEM Workshop and a homeownership workshop.

*V. Social Justice and Human Rights Initiative-*These initiatives address gender equality issues including: human trafficking and domestic violence, services for children with incarcerated parents, youth aging out of foster care and children in homeless shelters. Voter empowerment, access to technology, training of parents as advocates for educational and health care needs of children and support of the arts are emphasized. Since it's chartering and under the current initiatives between 2010-13, Upsilon Kappa Omega has sponsored the following programs: Youth aging out of Foster Care graduation, Bicycle Man Giveaway, Shop with the Sheriff's Christmas Giveaway, Donation of School Supplies, Domestic Violence Awareness, Bowl for the Cure, Care Center Makeover, Women's Empowerment Seminar and Financial Literacy Programs.

Karla Dunigan with International President Carolyn House Stewart at the 2012 Boule in San Francisco, California.

January 4, 2012

Alpha Kappa Alpha Sorority, Inc.
Upsilon Kappa Omega Chapter
P.O. Box 53421
Fayetteville, NC 28305

Dear Ladies of Alpha Kappa Alpha:

On behalf of the Second Harvest Food Bank of Southeast North Carolina, we would like to thank you for the recent donation. Your choice in partnering with the Second Harvest Food Bank of Southeast North Carolina shows your commitment to the well-being of the community and is something that you should take great pride in.

Your support yielded 148 pounds of donated items, with a value of $245.68, on December 10, 2011. You can be assured that the food items were distributed to many needy families within our service area. Your efforts helped us ensure that many individuals were able to have plenty of food throughout the holiday season.

We look forward to working with you on future endeavors and we greatly appreciate your commitment to the food bank, its mission, and the people we serve. Please contact me if we can assist you in any way at:

Patra Roberts
Tel: 910-485-6923 ext 104
Email: patra.roberts@ccap-inc.org

Sincerely,

Patra Roberts
Food Sourcing Coordinator

406 Deep Creek Road PO Box 2009 Fayetteville, NC 28312 | (910) 485-6923 | www.ccap-inc.org/foodbank
A division of Cumberland Community Action Program, Inc.

98

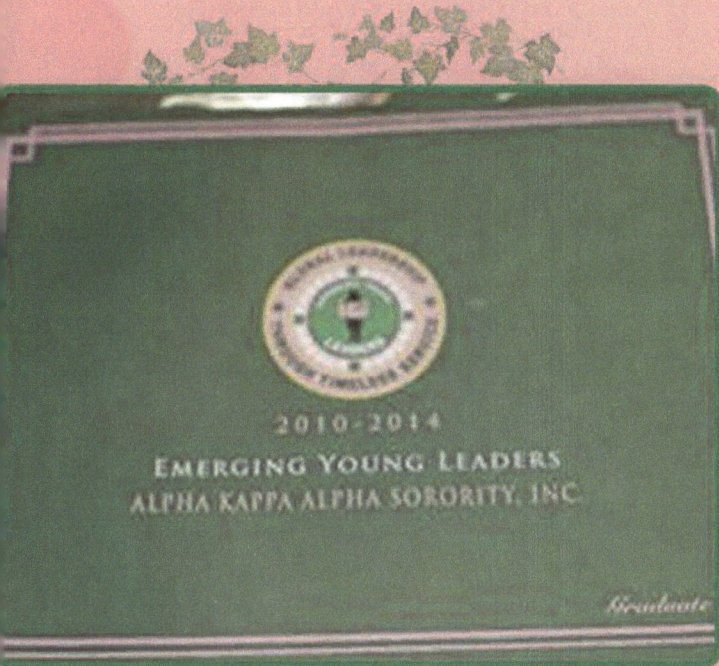

2013 EYL Graduates Celebrate!

Emerging Young Leaders Summer Retreat August 2013

Health Initiative-Asthma Awareness Camp

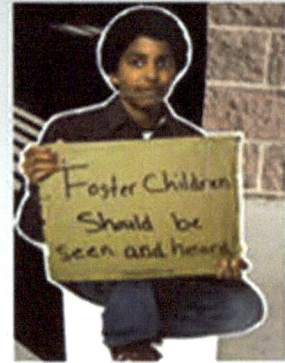

Social Justice & Human Rights

Economic Security-Habitat for Humanity

Internal Leadership Training Standards Retreat August 2013 at Camp Rockfish

Health Initiative-Assisted at the
MOM Dental Clinic, July 2013

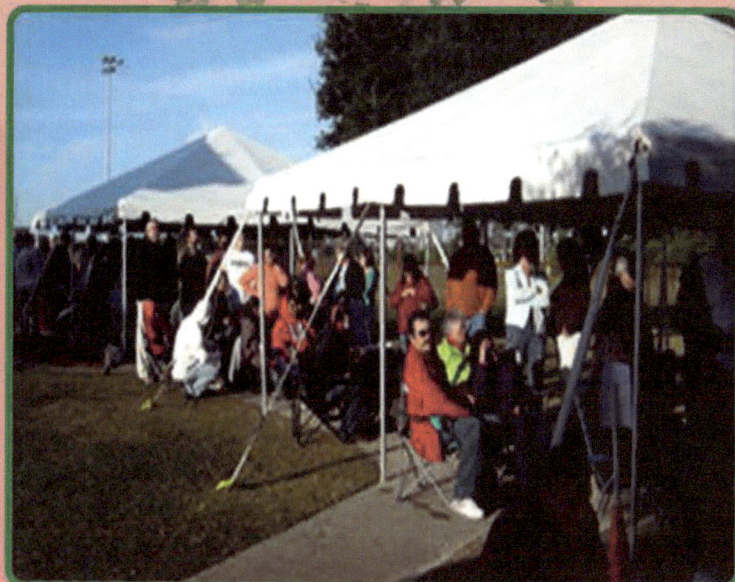
Mission of Mercy
Dental Clinic waiting area

Global Poverty-Fed over 250 hungry persons at Salvation Army
July 2013

Human Trafficking Seminar June 30, 2012

Alpha Kappa Alpha Sorority, Incorporated

UPSILON KAPPA OMEGA

June 15, 2012

RE: Human Trafficking Awareness Program (6/30 Documentary Screening)

The ladies of Alpha Kappa Alpha Sorority, Incorporated, Upsilon Kappa Omega chapter, are hosting a documentary screening of the film, *Very Young Girls*, to promote Human Trafficking awareness, prevention, and intervention of young women, ages 12 to 24. This event will be held on June 30, 2012 at the North Regional Library (855 McArthur Road, Fayetteville, NC 28311), from 3:00 PM – 5:30 PM.

Alpha Kappa Alpha Sorority, Incorporated, is an organization comprised of over 200,000 educated, poised, and professional women worldwide. Our commitment to our motto, "Service to All Mankind," charges us every year to raise awareness on issues that directly impact our community.

Youth-Young Adults, Parents, Educators and Churches are encouraged to attend (see attached flyer). Light refreshments will be served. Program will start promptly at 3:00 PM.

What to expect from the documentary and wrap-up session?

Very Young Girls is a documentary exposé on human trafficking that follows 13- and 14-year-old African-American girls. Using intimate interviews with the barely adolescent girls, the film gives a rare glimpse into how the cycle of street life begins for many young women. The film also documents the work of Girls Educational and Mentoring Services (GEMS), a recovery center founded and operated by Rachel Lloyd, a survivor of sexual exploitation. With the help of GEMS, many young women are given a chance to piece their lives back together. Through the use of unprecedented access to girls and pimps, the producers of the documentary hope to "change the way law enforcement, the media and society as a whole view sexual exploitation, street prostitution, and human trafficking that is happening right in our own backyard."

This program format utilizes the critically acclaimed documentary *Very Young Girls* as the backdrop for a probing and insightful discussion about Human Trafficking in the United States. After viewing the film, audience members will have the opportunity to ask questions, react to themes raised in the film, and respond to questions raised by the facilitators. Topics that will be discussed include:

- Stereotypes about girls involved in the commercial sex industry
- Relationship between child sexual abuse and commercial sexual exploitation of children
- Contradictions between laws that protect girls from sexual abuse/exploitation and those that criminalize these underage girls
- Specific types of services commercially sexually exploited youth require

If you have any additional questions, please contact Courtney Locus at (910) 494-6192.

Sincerely,
Chekea Hinton-Mack
Programs Chair

Karla Dunigan
President

Enclosure

P.O. Box 53241 • Fayetteville, NC 28305

Members of Upsilon Kappa Omega Chapter have found it rewarding to sponsor programs that benefit the community. Members are also encouraged to continue personal, professional and educational growth and development through opportunities offered by the sorority at the chapter, regional and international levels because it recognizes that adequate training is beneficial to chapter operations and effectively executing programs in the community.

With a focus on service in the community, Upsilon Kappa Omega Chapter continues to fulfill its initial vision and goals within the Fayetteville, Fort Bragg and Pope Army Airfield communities. Upsilon Kappa Omega Chapter will continue its mission of service with the development of a new mission statement and vision which further defines and captures its purpose in its quest to provide service to all mankind.'

Mission Statement

The dedicated LADIES of Upsilon Kappa Omega Chapter commit to being a welcoming chapter that strives to uphold our sisterly values while empowering others.

Vision Statement

SISTERS EMPOWERING LIVES BY A.C.T.S.

ASSISTING

COMMUNITIES

THROUGH

SERVICE

Postlogue
REFLECTIONS: MEMORABLE EXPERIENCES
Upsilon Kappa Omega

Arrie McAlister: Most memorable: December 1, 1996—Our chartering! This meant a lot to me because it was my desire to have a chapter in the area that would be inclusive to the military community, as well as surrounding communities and new ideas. Valeria Collins did not hesitate when I approached her with the thought of chartering a new chapter in the area. With her help and those first few [sorority members] who gave of their time and talents to form our interest group, we were on our way.

Lyndelia Wynn: 12/13/1998- the date I became an AKA.

Dia M. Collins: As the [president] for 2007-2008, I lead the chapter through its first on-site evaluation and represented the chapter during our Centennial Boule. I enjoy each Jazz on Top of the Town where we all get together and have a good time! I truly enjoyed the 2004 Boule where me, Arrie, Jackie, Sharon and Carolyn (I think) did a performance during the luncheon as an old school group.

Sharon D. Taylor: I have had several memorable experiences as a member of Upsilon Kappa Omega. The first was my initiation in 2001. The second was attending Boule 2004 and dressing up as Martha and the Vandellas with Afro wigs and sequined pink dashikis for entertainment during the MAR Luncheon. The third was when our chapter was hosting a cluster and for our invitation the chapter members dressed in pink and green BDU's with pink berets, and pink pumps, it was such a hit!

Amia Samica Randazzo: The [members]of UKO have been very welcoming as I've only been with the chapter for slightly over a year. I'm grateful and glad to be part of a chapter that's active as this and look forward to continuing to serve.

Rasheedah Parson: I'm two months new to the chapter, however, I enjoy everything I do with Upsilon Kappa Omega.

Lydia Berrios: I don't have one memory with UKO that resonates. When I think of UKO I think of the true sense of "sisterhood" that we represent; we are family in good times and bad. I am proud to say yes I am a member of Upsilon Kappa Omega. The presence we have in the community is incomparable to any other sorority in the Fayetteville or surrounding area. I am proud to have served in the various capacities I have served on behalf of Alpha Kappa Alpha Sorority and Upsilon Kappa Omega chapter, and proud to have named the newsletter the "Ivy View" during my term as [corresponding secretary].

Teresa C. Locus: One of my most memorable experiences with UKO is having my daughters to be initiated into the chapter.

Takeisha Parker-Wilson: I have only been in the chapter for three months. However, I am awaiting my most memorable experience in the chapter. I anticipate many throughout the year!

Antionette (Toni) Bennett: Upsilon Kappa Omega has always been a caring chapter, not only for members, but for the community. When we visited the Veteran's Hospital it touched my heart because so many Vets believe that people have just forgotten about them after they take the uniform off, but UKO remembers them often and that makes my heart proud.

Tamara Carter Woods: Attending the Boule in Florida [2004].

Karla P. Dunigan: My most memorable experience with Upsilon Kappa Omega was in my service as [president]. It was a tremendous learning experience and enabled me to develop great relationships within UKO and among other [AKA's] at the local, regional, and national levels.

Charlene Sumlin Cross: The chartering experience.

Daisy M. Thompson: Hearing the name of the new chapter revealed at the reception in December, 1996. UKO's visit off Old Wilmington Road. The residents thought we were there for prayer meeting so that's what we did!

Pamela Gainer: One of my most memorable experiences is when I had major surgery. Several members came to help me and my family during my recovery. Another experience as membership chair, I was able to assist this chapter in making sure new [members] embrace lifelong membership. They are all still financial and active.

Audrey R. Noble: My most memorable experiences with Upsilon Kappa Omega are singing the hymn and pledge. I am always reminded of why I joined this GREAT Sisterhood. It gives me this unexplainable feeling I'm sure our founders experienced as well.

Andrea Mial: [A] warm welcome at the 1st meeting…Arrie's continued personal calls and emails.

Chelsea Forbes: MIP [Membership Intake Process]   :D

Michelle Hawkins: [Mid-Atlantic] Regionals (Asheville, NC).

Kathy Hardy: Every experience has been a memorable one; however, my attendance at the 2012 [Mid-Atlantic] Regional Conference was the most memorable one.

Kristin Braswell: The Hands That Help Christmas Luncheons.

Desdy H. Paige: My most memorable experiences are (1) joining UKO in January 1998 (2) when Upsilon Kappa Omega Chapter did the invitational in 2005 in Williamston, NC for the 2006 Eastern Carolina Cluster that UKO would be hosting in Fayetteville, NC. It was so successful that Dr. Caroline Lattimore, Regional Director at the time, asked UKO to do a "Tribute to the Troops" in Arlington, VA. during the public meeting at the 2006 Mid-Atlantic Regional Conference.   We wore pink BDU's, pink berets and pink pumps.   That tribute was very well received by AKA's in attendance, the military community, and citizens from the area.

E. Rochelle Carter: When we went to [Northern Virginia] for regionals and wore our pink BDU's. Also Hands That Help.

Monica Stanford: When the chapter expressed concern, support and sympathy when my father passed away. Also, working on the Extreme Makeover Project [Jubilee House-2011].

Tracy Allen: The most memorable experience that I had with Upsilon Kappa Omega Chapter was the birth of "Sweets Sixteen" [MIP]. We were so sweet and divine. It was when I gained 15 new sisters to my life. I was number sixteen. The other most memorable event is when we went to cluster and regionals to perform in our BDU's. Those are moments that I will cherish forever.

Sharon H. Glover: I enjoyed the sisterly activities.

Monique D. (McAlister) McEachern: The chartering experience was most exciting for me. This chapter was my first graduate chapter since I graduated from UNC-G.

Valeria A. Collins: The road traveled from Harambee to UKO [Upsilon Kappa Omega]!

Appendix

Chapter's Officers 1997-2008

UKO Officers 1997

President-Valeria A. Collins
Vice-President-Carolyn McLaurin
Recording Secretary-Barbara Melvin
Assistant Recording Secretary-Twylla Willis
Financial Secretary-Charlene Sumlin
Treasurer-Shirley C. Greene
Corresponding Secretary-Shirley M. Evans
Hostess-Beverly Simmons
Door Keeper-T'Anya Johnson
Publicity Chairperson-Carla Collier
Historian-Renarta Clanton
Chaplain-Cheri Siler
Parliamentarian-Arrie McAlister (appointed)

UKO Officers 1998

President-Valeria A. Collins
Vice-President-Shirley Greene
Recording Secretary-LaDonna Howell
Financial Secretary-Charlene Sumlin
Treasurer-Twylla Willis
Corresponding Secretary-Shirley M. Evans
Hostess-Renarta Clanton
Door Keeper-Juanita Williams
Publicity Chairperson-Felicia Robinson
Historian-Beverly Simmons
Chaplain-Burma Anderson
Parliamentarian-Cheri Siler

UKO Officers 1999

President-Charlene Sumlin
Vice-President-Carolyn McLaurin
Recording Secretary
Assistant Recording Secretary
Financial Secretary
Treasurer-Sharon Wilson
Corresponding Secretary-Shirley Evans
Hostess-Vinette Gordon
Door Keeper-Arrie McAlister
Publicity Chairperson-Karen Briggman
Historian-Daisy Thompson
Parliamentarian-LaDonna Howell

Committees and Chairs

Programs/Fundraising-Wendy McManus
Gilmore/Carolyn McLaurin
Budget and Finance-Sharon Wilson
Public Relations-Karen Briggman
Bylaws-LaDonna Howell
Standards-Joyce Barr
Membership-Shirley Evans
Hospitality/Protocol-Vinette Gordon
Archives-Daisy Thompson
Connections/Political Action-Beth Hall
PIMS-Angela Newble
Cultured Pearls-Desdy Paige
Scholarship/Awards-Arrie McAlister

Chapter's Officers 1997-2008

UKO Officers 2000

President-Carolyn McLaurin
Vice-President-Shirley Evans
Recording Secretary-Beverly Simmons
Assistant Recording Secretary-Dionne Hall
Financial Secretary-Angela Newble
Treasurer-Sharon Wilson
Corresponding Secretary-Barbra Parker
Hostess-Leslie Brickhouse
Door Keeper-Arrie McAlister
Publicity Chairperson-Michelle Graham
Historian-Andrea Jackson
Chaplain-Valeria Collins
Parliamentarian-Anne Brinkley

Committees and Chairs

Programs/Membership-Shirley Evans
Budget and Finance-Sharon Wilson
Hospitality-Leslie Brickhouse
Public Relations-Michelle Graham
Bylaws-Valeria Collins
Standards-Shirley Greene
Archives-Daisy Thompson
Fundraising-Sharon Glover
Political Action/Connections-Beth Hall
PIMS-Angela Newble
Cultured Pearls-Desdy Paige
Standards-Shirley Greene

UKO Officers 2001

President-Shirley Evans
Vice-President-Arrie McAlister
Recording Secretary-Jeanette Avery
Assistant Recording Secretary-
Revella Lynn Surles
Financial Secretary-Beverly Simmons
Treasurer-Sharon Wilson
Corresponding Secretary-Carolyn McLaurin
Hostess-Donyell Dawson
Door Keeper-Juanita Williams
Publicity Chairperson-Michelle Graham
Historian-Desdy Paige
Chaplain-Cheri Siler-Mack
Parliamentarian-Karla Dunigan

Committees and Chairs

Programs/Membership-Arrie McAlister
Budget and Finance-Sharon Wilson
Hospitality-Donyell Dawson
Public Relations-Michele Graham
Bylaws-Karla Dunigan
Archives-Desdy Paige
Fundraising-Daisy Thompson
Pan-Hellenic Representative-Carolyn McLaurin

Chapter's Officers 1997-2008

UKO Officers 2002

President-Myra Payne-Stokes
Vice-President-Sharon Wilson
Recording Secretary-Tamara Carter
Assistant Recording Secretary-
Wendy McManus
Financial Secretary-Barbra Parker
Treasurer-Sharon Taylor
Corresponding Secretary-Daisy Thompson
Hostess-Sharon Peterson
Door Keeper-Erica Fortenberry
Publicity Chairperson-Jacqueline Mardis
Historian-Desdy Paige
Chaplain-Gwendolyn Washington
Parliamentarian-Cheri Siler-Mack

Committees and Chairs

Programs-Sharon Wilson
Budget and Finance-Sharon Taylor
Public Relations-Michelle Graham
Membership-Arrie McAlister
Archives/Cultured Pearls-Lyndelia Wynn
Standards-Charlene Sumlin
Bylaws/Connections-Cheri Siler-Mack
Scholarship-Shirley Evans
PIMS-Erica Fortenberry
Fundraising-Daisy Thompson
Hospitality-Sharon Peterson
Pan-Hellenic Representative-Tamara Carter

UKO Officers 2003-2004

President-Arrie McAlister
Vice-President-Sharon Wilson (2003)
Dia Collins (2004)
Recording Secretary-Tamara Carter
Assistant Recording Secretary-
Wendy McManus
Financial Secretary-Barbra Parker
Treasurer-Sharon Taylor
Corresponding Secretary-Daisy Thompson
Hostess-Erica Fortenberry
Door Keeper-Jacqueline Mardis
Publicity Chairperson-Linda Lundie
Historian-Robbie Richardson
Chaplain-Gwendolyn Washington
Parliamentarian-Karla Dunigan

Committees and Chairs

Programs-Sharon Wilson (2003)
Dia Collins (2004)
Budget and Finance/Membership-
Sharon Taylor
Standards-Jacqueline Mardis
Hospitality-Erica Fortenberry
Archives-Robbie Richardson
Scholarship/Awards-Shirley Evans
Byaws-Karla Dunigan
Pan-Hellenic Representatives-
Tamara Carter/Erica Fortenberry
Music-Terri Knight
Cultured PEARLS-Cheri Siler-Mack
Public Relations/Publicity-Linda Lundie
Fundraising-Daisy Thompson

Chapter's Officers 1997-2008

UKO Officers 2005-2006

President-Cindy White
Vice-President-Dia Collins
Recording Secretary-Arrie McAlister
Assistant Recording Secretary-
Sherrine McCovery
Financial Secretary-Jacqueline Mardis
Corresponding Secretary-Daisy Thompson
Treasurer-Sharon Taylor
Hostess-Tonisa King
Door Keeper-Kimberly Whitfield
Publicity Chairperson-Lyndelia Wynn
Historian-Erica Hudson
Chaplain-Carolyn Williams
Parliamentarian-Cheri Siler-Mack

Committees and Chairs

Programs-Dia Collins
Budget and Finance-Sharon Taylor
Membership-Erica Fortenberry
Standards-Sharon Wilson
Hospitality-Tonisa King
Archives-Erica Hudson
Bylaws-Cheri Siler-Mack
Public Relations/Publicity- Lyndelia Wynn
Fundraising-Daisy Thompson
Music-Terry Knight
Pan-Hellenic Representatives-
Tamara Carter/Wendy McManus
/Erica Fortenberry
Technology-Sherrine McCovery
Anniversary Celebration-Daisy Thompson

UKO Officers 2007-2008

President- Dia Collins-Jackson
Vice-President-Sherrine Anderson
Recording Secretary-Daisy Thompson
Assistant Recording Secretary-Karla Dunigan
Financial Secretary-LaRue Kirkpatrick-Kerr
Corresponding Secretary-Arrie McAlister
Treasurer-C. Michelle Benson
Hostess- Julia Foreman
Door Keeper-Lavondra Pye
Publicity Chairperson-Tanesha Hendley
Historian-Jacqueline Mardis
Chaplain-Shirley Evans
Parliamentarian-Meleisa Rush-Lane

Committees and Chairs

Programs-Sherrine McCovery-Anderson
Standards-Chekea Hinton-Mack
Membership-Ellenita Golding
Hospitality-Julia Foreman
Scholarship-Angela Newble
Budget and Finance-C. Michelle Benson
Archives-Jaqueline Mardis
Bylaws-Meleisa Rush-Lane
Public Relations/Publicity-Taneisha Henley
Fundraising-Tonisa King
Connections-Nuschat Thomas
Technology-Daisy Thompson
Music-Michelle Hawkins
Centennial-Sherinne McCovery-Anderson

Chapter's Officers 2009-2014

Chapter Officers for 2009 - 2010
President-Sherinne Anderson
Vice President-Vikki Andrews
Recording Secretary-Andrea Royster
Assistant Recording Secretary-Terri Knight
Financial Secretary-Pamela Perkins-Burch
Assistant Financial Secretary-LaTonya Evans
Treasurer-Michelle Benson
Assistant Treasurer-Sharon Taylor
Corresponding Secretary-Linda Lundie
Hostess-Christine Campbell
Door Keeper-Arvita Callejas
Parliamentarian-Karla Dunigan
Ivy Leaf Reporter- Juelle McDonald
Historian-Jacqueline Mardis
Chaplain-Cheri Siler-Mack

Committees and Chairs
Programs-Vikki Andrews
Standards-Jurlonna Walker (2009)
Desdy Paige (2010)
Membership-Sharon Taylor
Scholarship-Julia Foreman
Fundraiser-Monica Standford
Pan-Hellenic-Tamara Carter
Connections-Latonya Evans
Technology-Elaine Atherton
Music-Sametris McKenney
Attire-Melissa Wells
Welcome-Carlotta Ray
Cultured Pearls-Chekea Hinton-Mack
Philanthropic-Rada Taylor
Protocol-Arrie McAlister
Archives-Jacqueline Mardis

Chapter Officers 2011-2012
President-Karla Dunigan
Vice-President-Chekea Hinton-Mack
Recording Secretary-Angela Carr-Finch
Assistant Recording Secretary-
Shavoka Douglas
Treasurer-Sharon Taylor
Assistant Treasurer-Dia Collins
Financial Secretary-Melissa Wells
Assistant Financial Secretary-Tracy Allen
Corresponding Secretary-Lydia Berrios
Parlimentarian-Teresa Locus
Door Keeper-Audrey Noble
Hostess-Lavondra Pye
Publicity Chair-Christine Campbell-Moore
Chaplain-Jacqueline Mardis
Historian-Desdy Paige

Committees and Chairs
Programs-Chekea Hinton-Mack
Membership-Pamela Perkins-Burch
Scholarship-Juelle McDonald
Fundraising-Andrea Royster
Standards-Sharon Wilson
Protocol-Arrie McAlister
Connections-Chekea Hinton-Mack
Technology-Benita Powell
Philanthropic-Vondra Mullino
Cultured Pearls-Dia Collins
EAF/Mentorship-Sherrine Anderson
Pan-Hellenic Representative-Wendy Lapsley
Music-Juanita Williams
Archives-Desdy Paige

Chapter's Officers 2009-2014

Officers and Committee Chairs 2013-2014

President-Dia Collins
Vice President-Pamela Gainer
Recording Secretary-Audrey Noble
Assistant Recording Secretary-Amia Randazzo (2013); Takeisha Wilson (2014)
Financial Secretary-Christine Campbell-Moore
Assistant Financial Secretary-Antionette Bennett
Treasurer-Sherinne Anderson (2013); Monica Rosario (2014)
Assistant Treasurer-Terri Knight
Corresponding Secretary-Monica Mason
Hostess-Melissa Wells
Door Keeper-Sharon Taylor
Public Relations-Tracy Allen
Historian-Desdy Paige
Chaplain-Juelle McDonald
Parlimentarian-Sharon Wilson

Committees and Chairs

Programs-Pamela Gainer
Fundraising-Lydia Berrios
Educational Advancement Foundation (EAF)-Karla Dunigan
Standards-Toni King
Pan-Hellenic Representative-Wendy Lapsley
Philanthropic-Teresa Locus
Membership-Arrie McAlister
Emerging Young Leaders- Joann Morton (2013); Toni King (2014)
Cultured Pearls-Takeisha Parker-Wilson
Protocol-Sharon Peterson
Scholarship-Rasheedah Parson
Technology-Benita Powell
Connections-Andrea Royster
Bylaws-Sharon Wilson
Archives-Desdy Paige
Music-Michelle Hawkins

UKO Membership 2013

Tracy Allen	Juelle McDonald
Sherrine Anderson	Sametris McKenney
Antionette Bennett	Christina McKoy
Lydia Berrios	Andrea Mial
Adrienne Bowman	Joann Morton
Trisha Bradley	Vonda Mullino
Kristin Braswell	Audrey Noble
Latonya Brown	Erica Noble-Mims
Kathy Brown-Bowen	Desdy Paige
Arvita Callejas	Takeisha Parker-Wilson
Christine Campbell-Moore	Sharon Peterson
Cynthia Carrol	Rasheedah Parson
Angela Carr-Finch	Benita Angel Powell
Rochelle Carter	Marva Powell
Tamara Carter Woods	Shanee Pratt
Dia Collins	LaVondra Pye
Charlene Cross	Amia Randazzo
Rasheeda Daniel	Carlotta Ray
Shirlisa Daniels	Serena Ravenell
Shavoka Douglas	Monica Rosario
Karla Dunigan	Andrea Royster
Dionne Evans	Cheri Siler-Mack
Chelsea Forbes	Monica Stanford
Pamela Gainer	Sharon Taylor
Pamela Gregg-Devose	Shani Thompson
Kathy Hardy	Melissa Wells
Michelle Hawkins	Carolyn Williams
Chekea Hinton-Mack	Juanita Williams
Gabrielle Holt	Sharon Wilson
Jan Johnson	Shanita Wooten
Robyn Johnson	Joslyn Wright
LaToya Kearns	Lyndelia Wynn
Toni King	Jennifer Young
Terri Knight	
Wendy Lapsley	
Stephanie Locus	
Teresa Locus	
Jacqueline Mardis	
Mykela Marshall	
Monica Mason	
Arrie McAlister	

UKO Membership Intake Process (MIP)

The FIRST-1998
Fatima Muhammed
Lyndelia Wynn
Leslie Brickhouse
Dionne Hall
Kathey Willis
Revella Lynn Surles
Michelle Graham
Xavier Williams
Beth Hall
Anne Brinkley
Jeanette Avery
Barbra Parker
Angela Whitson
Robin Browder-Swinson

Tenacious Ten-2001
Erica Fortenberry
Alicia Hill
Charlene McLean
Terri Knight
Gwendolyn Washington
Sharla Evans
Chaundra Taswell
Sharon Taylor
Jacqueline Mardis
Sharon Peterson
Nu Edition "And One"
Cynthia Brown

Teachy Two-2002
Stephanie Carver
Linda Lundie

Eleven Enchanting Connections-2003
Lena Williams
Kathy Bowen
Kimberly Whitfield
Walthea Corbiz
Sandra Thurman
Willie Adams
Erica Hudson
Tamika Sanchez-Jones
Vanessa O'Neal
Toni King
Chandra Evans

Sweets Sixteen-2005
Shandra Cofield
Julia Foreman
LaRue Kirkpatrick-Kerr
Nikki Massey
GeRita Johnson
Connie King
E. Rochelle Carter
Bonnie Anderson
Charmayne Morrison
Angela Carr-Finch
Jessica Brayboy
Christal Evans
Christine Campbell
Kristin Sharp
Lavondra Pye
Tracy Allen

Eighteen Scents of Sophistication-2007
Latonya Evans
Shameicha Wade
Shayla Watson
Melissa Wells
Celeste Ward-Bey
Erica Noble- Mims
Latoya McLean
Vondra Mullino
Elaine Atherton
Juelle McDonald
Labecca McNeill
Shinicka Spears
Beverly Sanders
Sametris McKenney
Peggy Jones
Kim Young
Chanee Lee
Latonya Brown

'Til the End of Time-2011
Robyn Johnson
Courtney Locus
Kathy Hardy
Antoinette Bennett
Chelsea Forbes
Dionne Evans

Luxurious Eight-2013
LaToya Kearns
Natasha Schroedel
Shirlisa Daniels
Stephanie Locus
Rasheeta Daniel
Cynthia Carroll
Jennifer Young
Joslyn Wright

Bibliography

AKA Style Manual: A Quick Reference for Sorority Publications. Connie Lynne Cochran, Editor in Chief, 5-14. *Ivy Leaf Magazine. Chicago. Alpha Kappa Alpha Sorority, Inc. 2011.*

Alpha Kappa Alpha Sorority, Incorporated. A Legacy of Sisterhood and Service-Founded 1908. www.aka1908.com.

Alpha Kappa Alpha Sorority, Incorporated. Upsilon Kappa Omega. Fayetteville/Fort Bragg/ Pope Army Airfield, NC. http://www.ukoaka1908.com.

'Alpha Kappa Alpha Sorority, Inc, Upsilon Kappa Omega Chapter, recently announced its 2012 scholarship recipients…" *Fayetteville Observer/Saturday Extra.* October 6, 2012.

'Alpha Kappa Alpha Sorority, Upsilon Kappa Omega Chapter recently welcomed new members…" *Fayetteville Observer-Times*/December 19, 1998.

Bouvier, Karen LaCaire." Pulling Together. Sorority's newest chapter turns to military population." *Fayetteville Observer-Times.* February 1, 1997.

'Cheers and Jeers." *Fayetteville Observer. January, 2011.*

"Eye on the Community." *Fayetteville Observer/Saturday Extra.* July 9, 2005.

"Eye on the Community." *Fayetteville Observer-Times*/February 6, 1999.

Fayetteville-2011 American City Video- YouTube. http:/www.youtube.com/watch/?vzYP53c3a-cD4. May 26, 2011.

Fayetteville Named All American City for a Third Time: WRAL.com. http://wral.com/news/state/story/9729663/. June 15, 2011.

*Fayetteville, NC-*Wikipedia, the free encyclopedia. http://en.wikipedia.org/wiki/Fayetteville,_North_Carolina.

*Fort Bragg-*Wikepedia, the free encyclopedia. http://en.wikipedia.org/wiki/FortBragg.

Fort Bragg, NC. /Facebook. https://www.facebook.com/fortbragg,nc.

"Fund-raising concert jazzes up festivities." *Fayetteville Observer-Times*/May 2, 1999.

Gordon, Vinette. "Womack unveils the Caring Touch system." *Womack Army Medica Center. Growing with Fort Bragg and our community.* Quarterly Newsletter-January-February-March 2012. Pg 2.

Huntington, Sam. *Fayetteville, The All American City. Article Source,* http://Ezinarticles.com.

Luss, Rhonda, MAR Technology Chairman. Email. *Congratulations Upsilon Kappa Omega. March 25, 2013.*

Lyle, Ethel Hedgeman. *Musings of a Founder.* Robertann B. Cuthbert, Editor. Ivy Leaf Vol 12 No.1 March (1934): 24. http://akawebnet.aka1908.net.

Mardis, Jacqueline. *Spanning the Sands of Time.* 2008.

Marvelous Mid-Atlantic Region. Alpha Kappa Alpha Sorority, Inc. Serving North Carolina and *Virginia/Global Leadership Through Timeless Service.* http://www.midatlanticaka.org.

McNealey, Earnestine Green, editor. "No. 108 in Mid-Atlantic." Ivy Leaf 75, No.1. Spring (1997): 30.
McNealey, Earnestine Green. *Pearls of Alpha Kappa Alpha: History of America's First Black Sorority.* Chicago: Alpha Kappa Alpha Sorority, Incorporated, 2010.

McNealey, Earnestine Green. *Timeless History Guide,* 4-12. Chicago: Alpha Kappa Alpha Sorority, Incorporated, (November) 2010.

McNealey, Earnestine Green. *Writing Timeless History,* 5-15. Chicago: Alpha Kappa Alpha Sorority, Incorporated, (March), 2011.

Pope Field- Wikipedia, the free encyclopedia. http://en.wikipedia.org/wiki/Pope_Field. *Pope Field. The Official Website of Pope Field.* http://www.pope.af.mil/

Pritchard,Catherine. Shop with the Sheriff. Kids treated to presents. *Fayetteville Observer/* December 2, 2012.

What's Next? Publishing Timeless Histories, 3-8. Chicago, Alpha Kappa Alpha Sorority, Inc. October 23, 2012.

Upsilon Kappa Omega Chapter of Alpha Kappa Alpha Sorority, Inc. http://www.facebook.com/ukoaka1908.

Index